The One Another Project

God's Strategy for Building His Church
and Conforming His Children into the
Image of His Son

Wayne Hoag

PRESS

Dedication

This book is dedicated to the Body of Christ at Sierra Bible Church in Truckee, CA. Being your shepherd for these past twenty years has taught me much about how God uses the members of His Body, the local church, to shape and mold His people into the image of His Son.

Acknowledgments

This book would never have come to print if it were not for several individuals whom God used to encourage me to turn ten sermons into a manuscript. There were many starts and stops along the way. Every time I let the project sit for a season another would come along and challenge me to take the next step. Thank you Mike and Patti Klayko, you were the first to suggest that the One Another Project sermons be made available in printed form and put the tools in my hands to make it happen. Thank you Bill and Darla Whitehead for your encouragement and help to get the manuscript edited. Thank you Doc and Mary Gelso for the gentle nudges and support that helped me take the final steps to publication. Thank you Sandy for being not only my partner in life but also in ministry. Your love, prayers and support are truly the wind beneath my wings. Thank you Lord Jesus for allowing me the privilege of playing a part in Your divine plan.

Table of Contents

Introduction

—ɷ—

Galatians 6:22-23, lists what is known as the Fruit of the Spirit. They are love, joy, peace, patience, kindness, goodness, faithfulness, gentleness, and self-control. These describe the character qualities of our Lord Jesus. Those who walked with Him would have sensed these traits emanating from His person. As Christians, filled with the Holy Spirit, others ought to discern these character qualities in our lives as well.

I would like to introduce you to what I am going to call "The Fruit of the Fruit of the Spirit." The essence of this "Fruit of the Fruit" is found in twenty-nine "one another" admonitions throughout the New Testament. The practice of these "one another" admonitions is the Fruit of the Spirit in action. And just as the Fruit of the Spirit depends upon a supernatural impartation to be manifested; so does the Fruit of the Fruit of the Spirit.

A few years ago while preaching through the Acts of the Apostles, I was awakened as never before to the interactions of the Jerusalem Church. I began to see that part of the secret of the power of their testimony was the way they related with and treated one another. The early chapters of Acts tell of a people that sacrificed for one another, fellowshipped, worshiped, and dwelt in one accord with one another. As a result, "Everyone kept feeling a sense of awe..." (Acts 2:43), "And the Lord was adding to their number day by day those who were being saved" (Acts 2:47), "...the people held them in high esteem" (Acts 5:13).

While pondering these things about the early church I began to compare it with the present day church in America. I had to ask myself, "Are we seeing these evidences today, evidences that have the power to make the world outside of the church sit up and take notice?" Can it be said of our churches, "There was not a needy one among them?" Are we seeing brothers and sisters in Christ as devoted to another as they were in Jerusalem?

As I prayed and pondered, I sensed God leading me to take the congregation that I pastor through the "one another" passages of the New Testament. It was as if He said to me, "My people need to come to an understanding of their vital need of one another. They need to understand that the koinonea (fellowship) of the New Testament was about being as committed to one another as they were to Jesus."

As Christians, we share a love for Christ's church and a love for the fellowship of the saints, but do we truly sense a deep need for one another and understand the vital part that the body of Christ plays in the shaping and maturing of each individual saint?

When I came to faith in Christ in 1972, the lyrics of one popular song of the Jesus Movement of that time were, "Me and Jesus got our own thing going, me and Jesus got it all worked out. Me and Jesus got our own thing going; we don't need anybody to tell us what it's all about."[1] I fear that today, we see that sentiment played out all too often in the church.

As I began to share with others what God had laid on my heart and how I felt that He was leading me to take the church through the "one another" admonitions of the New Testament, I was met with many interesting responses. Such as, "Why would you want to do that? We need to hear sermons of relevance and purpose for today." Or, "Isn't there something more interesting to preach on than that?" But as I preached through these admonitions the congregation found that these sweet little three to eight word admonitions have teeth in them. Through these words the Holy Spirit began performing open heart surgery in our midst.

As we moved into the heart of these admonitions, I heard more than once, "I can't do this." That is exactly the response the Holy Spirit wished to raise, for that is the bottom line truth of the matter. We cannot produce this fruit in our own strength.

I also found a difference between "I can't" and "I won't," with the latter being the most troublesome of the two. The "one another" admonitions are not suggestions, they are commands. The Lord does not call us to do them because we feel like it; rather, He calls us to do them out of obedience to Him.

Oswald Chambers wrote, "All God's revelations are sealed until they are opened to us by obedience. You will never get them by philosophy or thinking. Immediately you obey, a flash of light comes. Obey God in the thing that He shows you, and instantly the next thing is opened up. One may read volumes on the work of the Holy Spirit, when five minutes of drastic obedience would make things as clear as a sunbeam."[2]

I am convinced that God desires to see His children manifest the Fruit of the Fruit of the Spirit both in the church and beyond its doors.

What I now write, I write with fear and trembling because the last thing that the Body of Christ needs today is another "how to do it" manual. The last thing the church needs is to hear from another preacher who thinks he has cornered the market on some "new truth." Rather, the church needs to hear from God and give heed to the issues nearest to His heart.

But somehow it still pleases God to do His speaking through the trembling lips of men by the foolishness of preaching (1 Corinthians 1:21). Only time will tell, if the compelling that I am feeling in my heart is a fanciful whim, or the compelling of God. If you have the courage to keep on reading, may God empower you to bear forth the Fruit of the Fruit of the Spirit.

The key verse for this study is Romans 12:5, "...so we, who are many, are one body in Christ, and individually members of one another." I pray that as you read you will grow in your understanding of just how much you need your brothers and sisters in Christ.

Chapter 1

LOVE ONE ANOTHER

—〰—

Of the twenty-nine "one another" admonitions found in the New Testament, the call to love one another stands as the foundation on which the others are built. Without it, the rest of them will fall into a heap of rubble.

On the church calendar, the day before Good Friday is known as Maundy Thursday. The word "Maundy" comes from the Latin phrase *dies manda ti*...The Day of Christ's Great Mandate.

During the course of that evening, Jesus stripped Himself to a loin cloth, picked up a basin and a towel and washed the feet of His disciples. Following this very awkward and uncomfortable event for the disciples, Jesus got dressed, reclined again at the table and spoke these words, "A new commandment I give to you, that you love one another, even as I have loved you, that you also love one another. By this will all men know that you are my disciples, if you have love for one another" (John 13:34-35).

This commandment is Christ's Great Mandate. Within it we find three significant statements to which we need to pay close attention:

The Command...Love one another.

How...............Even as Jesus has loved us.

Why...............That a watching world will know that we are His disciples.

The visible evidence that we are truly Christ's disciples is not our devotional life, our church attendance, our giving, our T-shirts, jewelry or bumper stickers, but the love that we display to one another, our brothers and sisters in Christ.

Later, that same evening, Jesus reiterated the Great Mandate. John 15:12 says, "This is My commandment, that you love one another, just as I have loved you."

How is Jesus asking us love one another? He said, "Just as I have loved you."

You might say, "That's impossible!" The only reason that it is impossible is because we choose to make it so.

Here is where the struggle begins with the one another admonitions, not so much a struggle between God's Word and our intellect but a struggle between God's Word and our will.

Oswald Chambers wrote, "God does not make us holy in the sense of character; He makes us holy in the sense of innocence; and we have to turn that innocence into holy character by a series of moral choices"[1]

In dealing with matters of the will, C.S. Lewis said, "Every time you make a choice you are turning the central part of you, the part of you that chooses (your will), into something a little different than it was before. And taking your life as a whole, with all your innumerable choices, all your life long you are slowly turning this central thing either into a heavenly creature or into a hellish one. Each of us at each moment is progressing to the one state or the other."[2]

When an individual is born again, their heart is cleansed and they are made new in the righteousness of Christ (see 2 Corinthians 5:21). It is then, through the actions of our will, that our character is developed along the line of our clean hearts.

God does not call us to do anything for which He has not made every provision through the Cross of Jesus and through the Holy Spirit that lives in every believer. The grace of God is sufficient for every detail of our lives. The Apostle Paul said, "I can do all things through Him who strengthens me" (Philippians 4:13).

What is the key that releases the power of God into our lives so that we might find the capacity to do His will? The key is obedience. Faith is a matter of do and acquire, not acquire and do. When, in faith, we obey the commands of God, contrary to how we feel about the command, God will release His power into our lives to complete that act of obedience.

Jesus said, "This I command you, that you love one another, just as I have loved you" (John 15:12). The command to love one another has nothing to do with how we feel about it. Rather, it is a call to obedience.

No writer of the Scriptures dissects more completely what Jesus meant by these words than the Apostle John. Let us listen to what he said about this great command, remembering that he was in the upper room on the night of Christ's Great Mandate.

"For this is the message which you have heard from the beginning, that we should love one another; not as

18

Cain, who was of the evil one and slew his brother. And for what reason did he slay him? Because his deeds were evil, and his brother's were righteous" (1 John 3:11-12).

Here, John reminds us of Christ's command but then follows it with instruction on how not to love one another, "…not as Cain, who slew his brother."

I find it interesting that John takes time and space in his letter to tell us what loving one another does not look like. And to do so he takes us to the Old Testament, Genesis 4. Here we read of two brothers, Cain and Abel. We read of the sibling rivalry that led to the murder of Abel by the hands of his own brother. John tells us not to love as Cain loved. Then, John goes on to tell us what love looks like.

"Do not marvel, brethren, if the world hates you. We know that we have passed out of death into life, because we love the brethren. He who does not love abides in death. Everyone who hates his brother is a murderer; and you know that no murderer has eternal life abiding in him. We know love by this, that He laid down His life for us; and we ought to lay down our lives for the brethren. But whoever has the world's goods, and beholds his brother in need and closes his heart against him, how does the love of God abide in him? Little children, let us not love with word or with tongue, but in deed and truth" (1 John 3:13-18).

What is the evidence that one has passed out of death into life? John says that the evidence is our love for the brethren.

What does John call the one who hates his brother? He says that he is a murderer.

This too follows the teachings of Christ. He taught that before sin is ever an action, it starts as a thought. He said that a man is guilty of adultery if he looks at a woman with lust in his heart (see Matthew 5:28). To covet another's goods is the same as stealing, while to hate another is akin to murder.

How do we manifest the abiding love of God in our hearts? John says that it begins with a willingness to lay down our lives for the brethren, just as Jesus laid down His life for us.

How are we to love? We are to love in deed and in truth. Here, John would agree with James when he wrote, "But prove yourselves doers of the word, and not merely hearers who delude themselves" (James 1:22).

Again, John states visible examples in his teaching on love. He tells us that if we see a brother or sister in need and possess the capacity to help and willingly do so, that the love of God abides in our hearts. But if we close our heart to the one in need, he asks, "How does the love of God abide in him?" (I John 3:17).

"And this is His commandment, that we believe in the name of His Son Jesus Christ, and love one another, just as He commanded us. And the one who keeps His commandments abides in Him, and He in him. And we know by this that He abides in us, by the Spirit whom He has given us" (1 John 3:23-24).

What is Christ's command? It is that we believe in Him and love one another.

Who is it that abides in Christ? It is the one who keeps His commandments.

John's words are clear and concise. He goes on to say that demonstrable love in a life will give evidence that one has truly been born again.

"Beloved, let us love one another, for love is from God; and everyone who loves is born of God and knows God. The one who does not love does not know God, for God is love. By this the love of God was manifested in us, that God has sent His only begotten Son into the world so that we might live through Him. In this is love, not that we loved God, but that He loved

21

us and sent His Son to be the propitiation for our sins. Beloved, if God so loved us, we also ought to love one another" (1 John 4:7-11).

Where does love originate? Love comes from God. What is the proof that one has been born of God? Everyone who loves is born of God.

How did God manifest His love for us? He sent His Son to be the propitiation (satisfaction) for our sins.

O, the wonder of God's love and the marvelous way He chose to manifest it to us. "For God so loved the world, that He gave His only begotten Son, that whoever believes in Him shall not perish, but have eternal life" (John 3:16).

The Apostle Paul spoke of the wonder of God's love for us when he said, "But God demonstrates His own love for us, in that while we were yet sinners, Christ died for us" (Rom. 5:8).

In Romans 8:32, Paul wrote, "He who did not spare His own Son, but delivered Him over for us all, how will He not also with Him freely give us all things?"

The wonder of this verse is that God gave *to* us and *for* us the very best, the most precious thing He could give…the life of His only begotten Son. What a gift!

When we begin to exchange gifts with another they grow in value over time as the friendship deepens. Not so with God. He went to the top shelf first and then asks, "Would it make any sense for Me to withhold from you any good thing if I gave my best first?"

John goes on to tell us that because we have received such a love, we in turn are able to love.

"We love, because He first loved us. If someone says, "I love God," and hates his brother, he is a liar; for the one who does not love his brother whom he has seen, cannot love God whom he has not seen. And this commandment we have from Him, that the one who loves God should love his brother also" (1 John 4:19-21).

Why do we love? Because God first loved us. We do not possess the capacity to love one another as God has called us to love one another unless we have first received His great love. As we walk in obedience to His word He grants us the capacity to love others as He has loved us.

While serving as a hospital corpsman in the U.S. Navy I worked in a large operating room. At that time the supervisor of the operating room was a woman that few cared for. She was easy not to like because she wasn't very likeable. She ruled the operating room as if it were her personal kingdom. She had few friends, even among her fellow nurses.

During that time, I was given the responsibility of ordering the surgical supplies for our unit. I was assigned an office directly across the hall from the supervisor's office. And to make matters even worse, all of my orders had to be reviewed, cleared and signed off by her.

I was a new Christian at that time and as I faced the task ahead, I could see no way that I could work under those conditions. I made this a matter of prayer and the leading I received from the Lord came in a manner that did not please me at all.

God required me to treat this woman with all the respect due her as one created by Him, the respect due her as a woman, and as a Naval officer. Reluctantly, I attempted to obey. As I obeyed, God did something I did not expect. He did not change her but He changed me; so much so that we became good friends.

As I began to treat my supervisor with courtesy and respect, she responded. Her rough edges became smooth and some of the barriers which she had been hiding behind began to come down.

In no way could I have loved this woman in my own strength. But God, on the heels of my obedience gave me the power to love and to love genuinely.

John goes on to say something else that gives us great pause. He tells us that if someone says he loves God yet hates his brother, he is a liar. Why? Because one cannot say He loves God, whom he has never seen and not love his brother whom he has seen (I John 4:20).

Years ago, an elderly minister spoke to me about this verse and its implications. He said, "One's love for God cannot exceed the love that one has for the one they love the least."

I have often pondered his words and have remembered them every time I read from God's Word the command to love another just as Christ loved me.

The Apostle Peter also exhorts us to love one another as an act of obedience to our Lord. "Since you have in obedience to the truth purified your souls for a sincere love of the brethren, fervently love one another from the heart" (1 Peter 1:22).

Here the apostle follows the admonition to love the brethren by telling us how, "...fervently and from the heart." This love is not one in words only, but a demonstrable love, genuine love, and fervent love.

In the same letter, Peter again stresses that we are to love one another fervently. First Peter 4:8 says, "Above all, keep fervent in your love for one another, because love covers the multitude of sins."

Where does Peter place the call to love one another? Above all!

What does he mean when he says that "love covers the multitude of sins"? To help us with this, we turn to the Old Testament, to the very verses that Peter may have had in mind when he wrote his epistle.

Proverbs 10:12 says, "Hatred stirs up strife, but love covers all transgressions." And again, from the same book we read, "He who covers a transgression seeks love, but he who repeats a matter separates intimate friends" (Proverbs 17:9).

Have you ever witnessed an action or heard the words of a brother or sister that distressed you, but you passed on to another? If we are walking in love the only person we will discuss the matter with is God.

When I was a youth pastor, our family dentist was a member of our church. He was a very wise man who deeply loved the Lord Jesus. He also loved the

Lord's people. And when he would witness such things or have someone try to tell him of such things, his response was, "Tell God on them." Telling God on them instead of others shows us one way we can cover a multitude of sin.

If we truly love one another from the heart we can accept one another's weaknesses, bear with one another's foolishnesses, and even endure another's unkindness.

Love does not excuse sin, but it does recognize that we are all in the same boat. We are all in process, daily being changed from glory to glory into the image of Christ (II Corinthians 3:18).

Elsewhere, the Apostle John exhorts us to pray for our brothers and sisters if we see them committing a sin not leading unto death. He said, "If anyone sees his brother committing a sin not leading to death, he shall ask and God will for him give life to those who commit the sin not leading to death" (1 John 5:16). When we can do this and not broadcast the sins of our brethren we protect the body of Christ and ourselves from the sins of gossip and slander; in effect, covering the multitude of sins. We then give God room to right the wrongs in the life of another.

Understand this, Peter does not ask us to condone or harbor blatant and unrepentant sin in the church. For the scriptures give us clear and definite guidelines for dealing with such sins.

How easy it is to say that we love one another. But God is more interested in how we display that love than in how much we talk about it. This kind of love was manifested in the early church and it opened the eyes of those living in Jerusalem following the Day of Pentecost.

My dear brothers and sisters, in the power of the risen Christ, let us love one another.

Questions to Ponder

Read 1 John 4:7-16

Love-Agape...unconditional, other-centered, faithful, reliable, abounding...it is God's love for us and God's love in us when we are born again.

Where does love originate?

What is the proof that one has been born of God?

How did God manifest His love for us?

Who initiated this love?

Do you need to do something to receive this love?

This passage comments on the one who knows God. What distinguishes the difference between knowing about God and truly knowing God?

John indicates that a key to loving is abiding. See also 1 John 3:23-24. Give some thought to the relationship between loving one another and abiding in God.

Can we find visible evidence in the life of one who is truly filled with God and abiding in Him as opposed to someone who is "working for Him"?

Read 1 Peter 4:8

How important is it to our God to live out of agape love?

Does Peter teach us that it is OK not to deal with sin?

Compare I Peter 4:8 to Proverbs 10:12, 17:9, what do you think?

What might you need to consider about yourself and/or your relationship with God through Jesus if you know that you don't have God's love for others in your heart?

What response/action can you identify in your own life as a result of this teaching?

Chapter 2

FORGIVE ONE ANOTHER

The Bible has much to say about forgiveness. "Be kind to one another, tender-hearted, forgiving each other, just as God in Christ has forgiven you" (Ephesians 4:32).

Once again the Scriptures present us with a "just as" admonition. In the last chapter we read the words of Jesus which called us to love one another just as He loved us. Now, He calls us to forgive one another in the same manner.

Before we venture much further let's take a moment and review the Great Commandments.

"But when the Pharisees heard that He had put the Sadducees to silence, they gathered themselves together. And one of them, a lawyer, asked Him a question, testing Him, 'Teacher, which is the great commandment in the Law?' And He said to him, 'You shall love the Lord your God with all your heart, and with all your soul, and with all your mind. This is the great and foremost commandment. The second is like it, you shall love your neighbor as yourself. On these two commandments depend the whole Law and the Prophets'" (Matthew 22:34-40).

How does one apprehend the capacity to love their brothers and sisters in Christ or their neighbor as they love themselves? We attain that capacity when the chief endeavor of our lives is to love the Lord our God with all our heart and with all our soul and with all our mind.

In the same way we discover that the love of God is the source of all true love, we will also discover the love of God is the source of all true forgiveness. In Christ alone we find the capacity to forgive one another, just as He has forgiven us.

In Colossians 3:12-13, the Apostle Paul wrote, "And so, as those who have been chosen of God, holy and beloved, put on a heart of compassion, kindness, humility, gentleness and patience; bearing with one another, and forgiving each other, whoever has a complaint against anyone; just as the Lord forgave you, so also should you."

In these verses, who does the Lord call to forgive? Those who have been chosen of God are called to forgive, just as we have been forgiven.

31

If you are not a child of God in Christ, these verses do not apply to you. But if you are, know this: forgiving one another reflects the true nature of the children of God. When you and I forgive one another, we reveal God's nature to a watching world.

In Matthew 18:21-22, we read an interesting discourse between Simon Peter and the Lord Jesus. "Then Peter came and said to Him, 'Lord, how often shall my brother sin against me and I forgive him? Up to seven times?' Jesus said to him, 'I do not say to you, up to seven times, but up to seventy times seven.'"

The rabbis of Jesus' day taught that one was to forgive the transgressions of another up to three times. That was their interpretation of Amos 1:6-15, in which we find these words, "Thus says the Lord, 'For three transgression of Gaza and for four I will not revoke punishment.'" This same phrase we find repeated three more times in the passage. It is also addressed to Tyre, Edom, and Ammon.

In his own mind, Peter was being quite generous in asking, "Shall I forgive up to seven times?" He had more than doubled that which was required by the rabbis.

Peter was not prepared for Jesus' response, "I do not say up to seven times but up to seven times seventy."

We must understand that Jesus did not lay out an exact standard that says 490 transgressions is the limit. He made that clear by the following example.

"For this reason the kingdom of heaven may be compared to a certain king who wished to settle accounts with his slaves. And when he had begun to settle them, there was brought to him one who owed him ten thousand talents. But since he did not have the means to repay, his lord commanded him to be sold, along with his wife and children and all that he had, and repayment to be made. The slave therefore falling down, prostrated himself before him, saying, 'Have patience with me, and I will repay you everything.' And the lord of that slave felt compassion and released him and forgave him the debt. But that slave went out and found one of his fellow slaves who owed him a hundred denarii; and he seized him and began to choke him, saying, 'Pay back what you owe.' So his fellow slave fell down and began to entreat him, saying, 'Have patience with me and I will repay you.' He was unwilling however, but went and threw him in prison until he should pay back what was owed. So when his fellow slaves saw what had happened, they were deeply grieved and came and reported to their lord all that had happened. Then summoning him, his lord said to him, 'You wicked slave, I forgave you all that debt because you entreated me. Should you not also have had mercy on your fellow slave, even as I had mercy on you?' And his lord, moved with anger, handed him over to the torturers until he should repay all that was owed him. So shall My heavenly Father also do to you, if each of you does not forgive his brother from your heart" (Matthew 18:23-35).

This slave owed a debt of 10,000 talents of silver to his master. One talent of silver represented 15 years of wages to the common laborer. Therefore, 10,000 talents of silver represented 150,000 years of wages.

Listen again to the words of the slave, "Have patience with me and I will repay you everything."

That statement was ludicrous! The debt was impossible for the slave to repay. So the slave did the only thing he could do, he fell on his face and began to beg for his master's mercy. And it worked! We then read, "And the lord of that slave felt compassion and released him and forgave him the debt."

Now, after being forgiven this incredible debt, you would have expected the man to be the most generous and merciful man in town. But that is not what we read of his actions.

The text tells us that he went out and found a fellow-slave who owed him 100 denarii, demanded payment, and then threw the man in prison when he could not pay.

We need to note here that one denarii represented a day's wage for the common laborer. So, 100 denarii represented 100 days of wages. Contrast the debts of the two men: 150,000 years wages as opposed to 100 days wages. 100 denarii could be carried in one's pocket. To move 10,000 talents of silver it would take 10,000 men each carrying 50 pounds of silver.

What is the point Jesus tries to make? We can't compare what God has forgiven us with what He asks us to forgive.

Witnesses quickly reported to the master the news of the ungrateful slaves dealing with one who owed him. The text tells us that the master had the slave thrown into a debtor's prison and turned him over to the torturers. Then Jesus added some very interesting words that we read in verse 35, "My heavenly Father will also do the same to you, if each of you does not forgive his brother from your heart."

How might this manifest itself in the life of a believer who refuses to forgive the transgression of another?

In 34 years of pastoral ministry I have had the opportunity to witness the ravaging and tormenting effects of unforgiveness. Let me explain.

I believe that when one is born again that they are forgiven of all their transgressions, past, present, and future. I believe this because of the witness of scripture. Colossians 1:13-14 says, "And when you were dead in your transgressions and the uncircumcision of your flesh, He made you alive together with Him, having forgiven us all our transgressions, having canceled out the certificate of debt consisting of decrees against us and which was hostile to us; and He has taken it out of the way, having nailed it to the cross."

Though our sins have been forgiven, the transformation of our character into the image of Christ requires a daily walk of obedience.

Remember the words of Oswald Chambers? "God does not make us holy in the sense of character; He makes us holy in the sense of innocence; and we have to turn that innocence into holy character by a series of moral choices."[1]

In the life of the believer, two things happen when we sin. First, we compromise our fellowship and intimacy with our Heavenly Father. Second, we become a victim of the Law of Consequence. I do not believe that God "gets us" when we sin, but because of the Law of Consequence, we get ourselves.

More than once, in my years as a pastor, I have had teenage girls come to my office and confess that they had been sexually promiscuous and had become pregnant. Upon that announcement I invited parents to the office where we all heard the tearful confession of the young girl. Those times usually ended by all of us kneeling before the Lord and witnessing her confession to the Lord. Upon that confession I assured the young woman that she was forgiven. But being forgiven did not mean that she was no longer pregnant.

That's where the Law of Consequence entered the scene. She would still have to carry that baby to term and make the heart rendering decision of whether to keep the baby or to place it for adoption. Her family, her church, and the public would witness the swelling of her stomach as the baby grew within her. Her secret would become visible, her sin would be known, even though she had found the forgiveness of God and her family.

Another example would be a criminal who surrenders his life to Christ while in prison. I guarantee you that when word of his conversion reaches the warden; the warden will not release him from his sentence. Even though his slate in heaven is clean, he must still pay a debt to society. This is the Law of Consequence.

As Christians, if we refuse to forgive one who has transgressed against us, we will be turned over to the torturing and tormenting effects of that unforgiveness. It does not matter who our grudge is against or why. If we hold on to it, it will lead to bitterness that will poison every fiber of our being, every aspect of our lives. Unforgiveness brings spiritual famine into our lives that will not only affect us but everyone in our circle. Only one thing can free us from the torturers, forgiveness that comes from the heart.

What does it mean to forgive one another from the heart? What does it look like? The following two examples speak to this matter in a powerful way.

"In 1946 Czeslaw Godleski was a member of a gang that roamed and ravaged the German countryside. On one farm they gunned down ten members of the Wilhelm Hamelmann family. Nine of the victims died, but Hamelmann himself survived his wounds.

Godleski was eventually arrested and sentenced to prison. After completing a 20 year prison term for his crimes, the state would not release him because he had nowhere to go. When Wilhelm Hamelmann heard of the situation, he asked the authorities to release Godleski into his custody. He wrote in his request, "Christ died for my sins and forgave me. Should I not then forgive this man?"[2]

In his book *Who Speaks for God?* Chuck Colson shared a riveting story of the power to forgive that one man found in Christ.

On February 9, 1960, Adolph Coors III was kidnapped and held for ransom. Seven months later, his body was found on a remote hillside. He had been shot to death. Adolph Coors IV, then fifteen years old, had lost his best friend.

The Coors case attracted nationwide attention. As suspect, Joseph Corbett, was apprehended, convicted and sentenced to life imprisonment in the Colorado penitentiary.

For years, through service in the Marine Corps and on into adulthood, Ad Coors harbored hatred for the man who had murdered his father. In fact, he said, "I would have done anything in my power to have killed him had I met him."

Then, in 1975, Ad became a Christian. Soon afterwards, he became part of a fellowship group which included a friend, Dale Morris. "Have you ever forgiven that man?" Dale asked Ad one day. Ad thought a moment and replied, "Sure, Dale. In my heart I have."

Dale pressed the question. "I'm not talking about that. I'm asking whether you have ever gone to him and told him you have forgiven him, and asked for his forgiveness that you have hated him for so long…"

It was during this exchange that Ad learned that Dale was regularly visiting the maximum security unit at Canyon City Prison, where the man convicted of killing Ad's father was confined. "Come with me when I go down next Wednesday," Dale exhorted his friend.

"That invitation hit me right in the pit of the stomach," Ad remembers. "There have been few tougher decisions in my life." Three weeks later,

Ad made his decision. Dale made arrangements for him to visit Joseph Corbett.

The men arrived at the prison only to learn that the convict had refused to see them. "The funny thing," Ad now recounts, "is that I wasn't relieved, I was disappointed." So he left Corbett a Bible and inscribed it as follows: "I'm down here to see you today. I am very disappointed that I can't. As a Christian, I have been commanded by our Lord and Savior Jesus Christ to ask for your forgiveness. I forgive you for the sins you have committed against our family, and I ask you to forgive me for the hatred I have had in my heart for you."

Later, when speaking to some friends, Ad explained that "Hatred is like the barrel of a shotgun that's been plugged. Pretty soon it's going to go off in your face. It hurts the hater more than the hated. It hurt me. It ate me alive, and it ate my family alive."

Remarkably, Ad also said, "Today I have a love for that man that only Jesus Christ could have put in my heart"[3]

As a Christian, don't ever say that you can't forgive. By the power of God's saving grace that forgave you, you can find the capacity to forgive another.

In his book *To End All Wars*, Ernest Gordon tells of the story of revival in a Japanese POW camp during World War II, a revival that sprang up as prisoners began to serve one another and to pray for their captors and tormenters and forgave them of their cruel deeds. In fact, following the war, many of those soldiers returned to Japan and the Far East as missionaries.[4]

It was said of King Henry VI of England: "He never forgot anything but injuries." Of Abraham Lincoln, Ralph Waldo Emerson wrote, "His heart was as great as the world, but there was no room in it for the memory of wrongs done to him." Charles Spurgeon said, "Cultivate forgiveness in your heart until your heart yields a fine crop of it."[5]

Forgiving one another has nothing to do with stirring up spiritual emotion for another; rather, it is the making of a moral decision that has the power to remove hatred and bitterness from our hearts.

When you forgive in the manner that Christ has commanded you to forgive, you will find that a captive has been set free, and much to your surprise you will find that the captive is you.

Questions to Ponder

Read Colossians 3:12-13

For one of those who have been chosen of God, what do we have to "put on" in order to forgive?

The heart of a man/woman produces the action of the person. What action is produced in these verses?

Was there a time in your life when you were particularly overwhelmed by the forgiveness of God?

Read Romans 5:8

When God forgives us, is He fully aware of our condition?

Does our forgiveness of someone mean that we must approve of their sin or condone their sin?

Charles Spurgeon said, "Cultivate forgiveness in your heart until your heart yields a fine crop of it." Webster's Dictionary gives four definitions of the word cultivate. Which ones fit Spurgeon's statement?

To prepare soil for the raising of crops.

To foster growth.

To encourage.

To make friends with.

How might this apply to a heart of forgiveness?

Jesus said, "If therefore you are presenting your gift at the altar, and there remember that your brother has something against you, leave your gift...and go your way, first be reconciled to your brother, and then come and present your gift" (Matthew 5:23-24).

When a breach occurs between you and another brother/sister in Christ, who is responsible to make the first move of reconciliation?

Romans 12:18 says, "If possible, as far as it depends on you, be at peace with all men." In light of that verse, what should be your posture when you experience a broken relationship between you and a brother/sister in Christ?

Chapter 3

CONFESS YOUR SINS TO ONE ANOTHER

What does James say about confessing our sins? "Is anyone among you suffering? Let him pray. Is anyone cheerful? Let him sing praises. Is anyone among you sick? Let him call for the elders of the church, and let them pray over him, anointing him with oil in the name of the Lord; and the prayer offered in faith will restore the one who is sick, and the Lord will raise him up, and if he has committed sins, they will be forgiven him. Therefore, confess your sins to one another, and pray for one another, so that you may be healed. The effective prayer of a righteous man can accomplish much. Elijah was a man with a nature like ours, and he prayed earnestly that it might not rain; and it did not rain on the earth for three years and six months. And he prayed again, and the sky poured rain, and the earth produced its fruit" (James 5:13-18).

Within this passage we find two "one another" ad-monitions. Though closely linked, we need to explore them separately.

"Therefore confess your sins to one another, and pray for one another, so that you may be healed" (James 5:16). Un-confessed sin erects two barriers, one between God and man and the other between man and man.

Of the barrier between God and man, the psalmist wrote, "If I regard iniquity in my heart, the Lord will not hear" (Ps. 66:18).

From *The Message*, translated by Eugene Peterson we read, "If I have been cozy with evil, the Lord will not listen."[1]

The words of James parallel the teachings of the Rabbis of his day. They taught that to find cures for the ills of life one needs to be right with God and right with their fellow man.

If a brother has been wronged, offended, or hurt by something we have done, our confession of such sin is not complete until we have personally confessed to the one we have wronged.

Listen to the words of Jesus from the Sermon on the Mount. "If therefore you are presenting your offering at the altar, and there remember that your brother has something against you, leave your offering there before the altar, and go your way; first be reconciled to your brother, and then come and present your offering" (Matthew 5:23 & 24). As important as worship is to our God, He says that he will not receive it if we have unresolved differences with another.

PRAY FOR ONE ANOTHER

"Therefore confess your sins to one another, and pray for one another, so that you may be healed" (James 5:16). This, my friend, is a call to intercession. James calls us to stand in the gap for another and intercede for others in their time of need.

Sometimes in my own life I have not been able to pray for myself. How thankful I have been that God raised up intercessors for me during such times.

One of the terms we hear when we talk to other Christians about prayer is the term "prayer closet." The prayer closet refers to that secret place in which we get alone with God. In that place we enter into our most intimate moments with our Heavenly Father. The prayer closet is not just a place we go to lay down the burdens of our lives, but also a place where we apprehend the burden of our Lord's heart for others.

Dr. Bob Pierce, founder of "World Vision," one day prayed, "Lord, break my heart with the things that break yours."[2] God answered that prayer and broke Dr. Bob's heart with the plight of the world's poor and suffering. As a result, World Vision was born and later on Samaritan's Purse.

That prayer represented a true act of intercession. In it Dr. Bob gave God permission to trouble his heart with the things that troubled God's.

One of the greatest benefits of interceding for others is that it gets our eyes off ourselves. In intercession we also experience one of the greatest expressions of loving one another. A beautiful picture of this we find in the Gospel of Mark.

"And when He had come back to Capernaum several days afterward, it was heard that He was at home. And many were gathered together, so that there was no longer room, even near the door; and He was speaking the word to them. And they came, bringing to Him a paralytic, carried by four men. And being unable to get to Him because of the crowd, they removed the roof above Him; and when they had dug an opening, they let down the pallet on which the paralytic was lying. And Jesus seeing their faith said to the paralytic, 'My son, your sins are forgiven.' But there were some of the scribes sitting there and reasoning in their hearts, 'Why does this man speak that way? He is blaspheming; who can forgive sins but God alone?' And immediately Jesus, aware in His spirit that they were reasoning that way within themselves, said to them, 'Why are you reasoning about these things in your hearts? Which is easier, to say to the paralytic, 'Your sins are forgiven'; or to say, 'Arise, and take up your pallet and walk'? But in order that you may know that the Son of Man has authority on earth to forgive sins'—He said to the paralytic—'I say to you, rise, take up your pallet and go home.' And he rose and immediately took up the pallet and went out in the sight of all; so that they were all amazed and were glorifying God, saying, 'We have never seen anything like this'" (Mark 2:1-12).

This story has been a favorite of mine since childhood; it is a story filled with adventure and risk and faith. It also paints a perfect picture of intercession. You might say, "How so?" Let me explain.

Four men became deeply concerned about the well being of a paralyzed friend. Apparently they had heard about Jesus and His ability to heal. But when they arrived at the house where Jesus was ministering they could not get inside. These men, not easily deterred or denied, went to the rooftop, tore away the tile shingles and lowered their friend through the roof and placed him at the feet of Jesus.

The words of healing that Jesus spoke He prefaced by a thought in His heart, "And Jesus seeing their faith..." Not the faith of the paralytic, the faith of his four friends!

When we intercede for others, when we pray for one another, our prayers resemble the ropes used to lower the paralytic before Jesus. Through prayer we lower individuals in need at the feet of Jesus, asking Him to consider their plight. And, "seeing your faith" the Lord moves in their lives.

When praying for others how should we offer up that prayer? With the same fervency you would desire from others if they prayed for you or a loved one.

Once again, hear the words of James, "Therefore, confess your sins to one another, and pray for one another, so that you may be healed."

I see two applications for the phrase, "so that you may be healed" First, prayer releases God's supernatural touch to an ailing brother or sister. In James 5:14, he exhorts us to call for the elders of the church so that they may anoint the sick with oil and pray over them the prayer of faith that has the power to heal and restore.

Second, I see a reward for the faithful intercessor. On more than one occasion, as I have committed to pray for another, God has brought healing and restoration into my own life, healing and restoration for which I was not specifically praying. It was as if God came into the back door of my life and applied His touch while I allowed my attention to be diverted in the direction of another.

BEAR ONE ANOTHER'S BURDENS

"Bear one another's burdens, and thus fulfill the law of Christ" (Galatians 6:2).

What is the Law of Christ? Jesus said, "This is My commandment, that you love one another just as I have loved you." James calls this the, "Royal Law" (James 2:8).

In the purest sense of the word, Jesus became our burden bearer when He went to the Cross. Of Him, Isaiah said, "Surely our griefs He Himself bore and our sorrows He carried" (Isaiah 53:4).

In a sense we are called to do the same for others. We find a wonderful example of this in Exodus 17.

"Then Amalek came and fought against Israel at Rephidim. So Moses said to Joshua, 'Choose men for us, and go out, fight against Amalek. Tomorrow I will station myself on the top of the hill with the staff of God in my hand.' And Joshua did as Moses told him to do, and fought against Amalek; and Moses, Aaron, and Hur went up to the top of the hill. So it came about when Moses held his hand up, that Israel prevailed, and when he let his hand down, Amalek prevailed. But Moses' hands were heavy. Then they took a stone and put it under him, and he sat on it; and Aaron and Hur supported his hands, one on one side and one on the other. Thus his hands were steady until the sun set. So Joshua overwhelmed Amalek and his people with the edge of the sword" (Exodus 17:8-13).

Hebrews 12:12-13 exhorts us to, "...strengthen the hands that are weak and the knees that are feeble..."

In many ways we can bear one another's burdens. We bear one another's burdens when we pray for one another. At other times God may call on us to help bear the material burden of a brother or sister. We can see this in the following passages.

Proverbs 3:27-28 advises us, "Do not withhold good from those to whom it is due, when it is in your power to do it. Do not say to your neighbor, 'Go, and come back, and tomorrow I will give it,' when you have it with you."

James 2:14-17 explains the relation between faith and works. "What use is it, my brethren, if a man says he has faith, but he has no works? Can that faith save him? If a brother or sister is without clothing and in need of daily food, and one of you says to them, "Go in peace, be warmed and be filled," and yet you do not give them what is necessary for their body, what use is that? Even so faith, if it has no works, is dead, being by itself."

John wrote, "But whoever has the world's goods, and beholds his brother in need and closes his heart against him, how does the love of God abide in him?" (1 John 3:17).

Recently someone told me of a man who always kept money tucked away in his wallet for a child who might need a pair of new shoes. The person who told me the story said that as long as they knew the man, no child in their church ever went without shoes. What a ministry!

Maybe God will call us to bear someone's burden of loneliness. Or we could bear the burden of a young couple who can't afford a babysitter and night out together, by volunteering to watch their children for them.

Burden bearing might be as practical as helping the elderly or a shut-in with some chores around their house, stacking firewood, shoveling snow, house repairs, etc.

Jesus said, "Greater love has no one than this, that one lay down his life for his friends" (John 15:13). Laying down one's life for a friend does not necessarily mean dying for another. Laying down one's life can be just the willingness to set aside some time, set aside your interests or your own needs, that you might bear the burden of another.

Would you be willing to pray and ask God for a heart that is more sensitive, ears that will hear, eyes that will see, the need that surround you so that you might become His vessel, willing to bear the burden of another?

Of the early church in Jerusalem, Acts 4:34 says, "For there was not a needy person among them..." The same should be said of us and could be said of us, if we will be willing to let God open our eyes, our ears, and our hearts to the needs of the brothers and sisters around us.

Questions to Ponder

Read James 5:16

What are the practical benefits of confessing our sins to one another?

Read Exodus 17:8-13

What was the ultimate result of Aaron and Hur's assistance to Moses?

How might this example apply to my intercessions for one another?

Read Isaiah 35:3 & Hebrews 12:12-13

Contemplate these two passages in light of bearing one another's burdens.

Dr. Bob Pierce prayed, "Lord, break my heart with the things that break yours." What might keep you from praying that prayer?

Can I think of anyone to whom I need to make confession, so that my confession before God is complete?

When you tell someone that you will pray for them, do you pray for them?

What keeps you from praying that God will lay the burden of His heart on mine?

Read and contemplate Matthew 25:31-46.

Chapter 4

BE DEVOTED TO ONE ANOTHER

Romans 12:9 says, "Let love be without hypocrisy. Abhor what is evil; cling to what is good. Be devoted to one another in brotherly love; give preference to one another in honor; not lagging behind in diligence, fervent in spirit, serving the Lord."

The King James Bible reads a bit differently. It says, "Be kindly affectioned to one another in brotherly love."

I have wrestled with this line because something interesting here becomes significant. This phrase admonishes us to love one another in two different ways.

There are two different Greek words for love in this phrase. I don't think a man can reveal to us what this really means, but only the Holy Spirit can reveal it to us. Twice God calls us to love one another but He calls us to love one another in two different ways.

The term "kindly affectioned" comes from the Greek word *storgos,* while brotherly love is from the Greek word *phileo. Storgos* refers to the affection between blood relatives. It speaks of the love of a parent for a child, and the child for the parent, a love between blood family members.

Phileo, the Greek word that is the root of the word Philadelphia (the City of Brotherly Love), denotes the love that we have for our fellow man. In this passage, we are told to have *storgos* for one another in our *phileo.* I'm not the wordsmith that can unpack this for you. I have been laying it before the Lord, asking Him to help me. "Give me some kind of vocabulary that would help me just grab a bit of it." Because I know that if we can take the tiny seeds of this into our hearts, God will allow it to germinate and begin to sprout and begin to grow, that it will grow into an understanding of what God would have us to see here.

Here is the best I've been able to do. "Be devoted to one another like a parent to a child as we walk side by side, brothers and sisters in Christ." That's the best I can do. The verse goes on to say, "...give preference to one another in brotherly love."

Let us consider two verses, and then I'll ask you a question. Luke 6:31 says, "Treat others the same way you want them to treat you." Then Matthew 7:12 says, "In everything, therefore, treat people the same way you want them to treat you, for this is the Law and the Prophets."

These verses explain what we call The Golden Rule. The Golden Rule calls us to "do unto others as you would have them do unto you." In its simplicity it might look like this. At one time or another all of us have given up a place in line, or a seat to another person, and hopefully at some time we've experienced the same graciousness from another.

A friend, who recently returned from Poland, told me about something that he witnessed again and again while riding the subways and the buses in that country. He witnessed younger people getting up, out of respect, and giving their seats to the elderly.

In our own land there was a time that when an elderly person entered the room, people would rise out of respect, hold the door open for another, let someone else take the first place in line, offer someone a seat. We do such things simply out of common courtesy, out of respect for one another. This type of respect ought to permeate the lives of Christians. Anybody can do it. You don't have to be a Christian to be polite, but we ought to epitomize this type of politeness.

We have lost a genteelness that used to be very evident. It seems like rudeness and pushiness tend to rule the day. We rarely hear the words "excuse me" when someone gets bumped into or pushed out of the way. We live in a world in a hurry to get someplace. It's a world in a hurry to just have their way, with little concern about being in another's way.

This contrast became evident when my wife and I lived in the South. Children seldom opened their mouths without a Yes, Sir, or Yes, Ma'am being spoken. Yes, sir. Yes, ma'am. Yes, please. No thank you. You have to pat the parents on the back who raise these children to respect their elders.

When growing up, I was taught that if an adult was speaking I was to keep silent. It did not mean that we, as children, never got a chance to talk. It simply meant that we did not interrupt others when they spoke, especially if they were older than us, not because they were bigger than us or anything else, but out of courtesy and respect.

Have you not experienced someone holding a door, somebody giving you a place in line, somebody saying please, thank you or excuse me, and you almost stop in your tracks because it feels like a breath of fresh air? Do unto one another, as you would have them do unto you.

As Christians, we are called to dial this principle up a notch. It's not just doing unto one another as you would have them do unto you; rather God calls us to give preference to our brothers and sisters in Christ, to be devoted to them and to give preference to them in honor.

Galatians 6:10 instructs us, "So then, while we have the opportunity, let us do good to all people, and especially to those who are of the household of the faith."

Isn't that interesting? If you have the opportunity today, do good to all people, and especially to those who are of the household of the faith. Here, the Apostle tells us, "Hey you, Christian, do good to people all the time when you have the opportunity to do good, and especially to your brothers and sisters in Christ." He calls us to extend an extra grace to one another, a grace and a courtesy that goes beyond what we have been called to extend to the world outside our door.

Romans 12:11 goes on to say, "…not lagging behind in diligence, fervent in spirit, serving the Lord."

When we honor one another, our primary service and honor is not to one another, but to the Lord. When

I walk with you in this manner and you with me, we serve Jesus first.

This principle resembles the admonition in Ephesians which tells husbands how to love their wives and wives how to love their husbands. God calls us to do that first and foremost, not for the benefit of our wife or husband, but in order to honor the Lord Jesus Christ. This passage means the same. When we walk with one another in this way, devoted to one another in brotherly love, giving preference to one another in honor, the Lord Jesus Christ first and foremost receives glory.

Think of Jesus' words in Matthew 25:40, when He said, "...as you did to one of these brothers of Mine, even to the least of them, you did it unto Me."

We need to look at one another as if our brothers and sisters are Jesus in disguise; because as we do or don't do to one another, we first of all do or don't do to Jesus. We either throw it in His face first, or we embrace Him first. We honor the Lord Jesus by the way we walk with one another.

Take heed to the exhortation found in Philippians 2:1-4, "Therefore if there is any encouragement in Christ, if there is any consolation of love, if there is any fellowship of the Spirit, if any affection and compassion, make my joy complete by being of the same mind, maintaining the same love, united in spirit, intent on one purpose. Do nothing from selfishness or empty conceit, but with humility of mind regard one another as more important than yourselves; do not merely look out for your own personal interests, but also for the interests of others."

"Regard one another as more important than yourself." Those are tough words in a day and age that exalts the self. Hardly a commercial on TV or an ad in a newspaper or magazine isn't about you feeling good, and you having yours first, and the most, and the best. It's all about me, me, me, and me. That's the way of the world, my brothers and sisters; it's the fruit of the flesh.

Here Paul talks about a call to Christian unity, and he says, "Be of the same mind. Maintain the same love for one another. Be united in spirit and intent on one purpose."

The Lord Jesus in His prayer the night before He died prayed three times, "Father, may they be one as You and I are one" (John 17:11, 21,22).

63

He then spoke of the power of such a witness. He told his disciples that such unity was evidence to a watching world that He is indeed the Christ, the Savior of the world.

As Christians, the way we live and deal with one another speaks volumes to the community in which we live. Through our actions and words they make their conclusions about Jesus. When we walk together in unity, our community sees evidence that Jesus is who He claims to be, the Messiah of the World.

Jesus said that when we endeavor to walk in unity with one another, something emanates from us that bear witness to the genuineness of the Lord Jesus Christ.

The Apostle Paul reiterates the theme here. Be of the same mind. Maintain the same love. Be united in spirit. Be intent on one purpose. How do we accomplish that? By doing nothing from selfishness or empty conceit, but with humility of mind regarding one another as more important than you.

The King James reads, "Let nothing be done through strife or vain glory" (Philippians 2:3). The Greek word for strife means electioneering. It means the promotion of self or the pursuit of recognition. Do you see me?

I have to be seen! Do you see me, do you see me? That's the way of the world. The apostle Paul says that's not supposed to be the way of the body of Christ. God calls us to walk with one another in humility.

The word humility strikes us hard in some ways because we tend to think of humility as mousy, weak, limp-wristed, lily-livered, and yellow-bellied. Nothing could be further from the truth. It takes a bigger man and woman to walk in humility. Humility means a willingness to rank under one another. Humility regards one another as more important than self.

I have seen this type of humility in the life of Dr. John Edmund Haggai, founder and president of the Haggai Institute. I have never been in Dr. Haggai's presence and heard him talk about himself. Whenever I have been with him, he has wanted to talk about me. Me! He makes others feel like they are the only person on the face of the earth. He is genuinely concerned with what's going on in the life of another. He's not always talking about what he's doing, saying, being and hoping. He asks, "How are you doing? Tell me about your family. Tell me about your church." You are almost in shock because it's so different from the way of the world.

Humility has nothing to do with our standing, our profession – rather it has everything to do with being willing to voluntarily rank under another, that they may be held in honor, that we may esteem them as more important than ourselves.

What would it be like if we were truly a people that were more concerned about seeing one another succeed rather than ourselves? What would that do to the church, if each time we gathered together we were more concerned about seeing one another being put to the forefront than ourselves; no one jockeying for the first place, but all of us endeavoring to lift one another to that direction and in that position? Can you imagine?

Yet that description is what Christ meant His body to look like. And such action became so powerful in the early chapters of the book of Acts that Jerusalem sat back with their collective mouths hanging open at what was happening in this people. They saw sacrifice, courtesy, and respect; not a needy one lived among them – they saw people who cared, and they cared sacrificially.

When we start talking about this type of sacrificial living, our flesh shudders. Do you know why? Because the devil has convinced us, or tried to convince us, that such an arrangement is filled with loss. But I want to tell you, that according to the Word of God, we will experience only gain. Not an ounce of loss is programmed in any of this.

If you were in a room with 100 people and they were all intent on esteeming others more important than themselves, the return of being in that room would be 99 to 1. If you are in a room with 100 people bent on loving one another as Christ loved His church, you will get back 99 times more than you give out. You can't lose in this! It's all gain! Not only for you and me, but for Jesus in his glory, and for a real, legitimate, powerful witness that will go beyond the walls of the church to a world that is watching. And the testimony becomes, "Oh, how they love one another."

A few years ago my wife and I were invited to a Christmas party at the home of a Christian brother. It just so happened that Sandy and I had also received an invitation to drop in at another party right across the street from this brother's house. It was at the home of a man who had been stopping by my office to talk about some of the problems of his life. I asked the brother if it would be alright if we stepped across the street for a few minutes. With his approval, we did.

Though we were dressed for a casual Christmas party we ended up at a black tie affair. The men were dressed in tuxedos and the women in evening gowns. Boy, were we out of place. The host graciously welcomed us in and tried his best to make us feel at ease.

We had just left a party that was celebrating our Lord's birth and the fellowship that we had in Him. Now, we are in a group of people impressed about one thing – themselves, and telling everybody else about it. The conversations were all about where they had traveled, how much they had made, how much they spent on their last car, their last vacation. It was the most hollow, shallow, nothing conversation in which I had been engaged. And nobody was impressed with anybody there except themselves, even though they tried very hard to be.

We stayed for a few minutes and then we went back across the street where we found true life. No one was wearing tuxedos or thousand dollar evening gowns, but there, we saw and experienced life. We heard laughter, and people cared about one another. No posturing, it was life in the Lord Jesus Christ.

My prayer for Christ's Church is that it might be a place where one-upmanship has died, that it is a place filled with people who endeavor to outdo one another in service and in love. And, if we must bump our heads, may it be as we bow in humble respect for one another. That's the cry and the prayer of my heart.

Be devoted to one another. Show preference to one another in honor, and in that, serving the Lord. Esteem one another as more important than yourselves.

Questions to Ponder

Read Romans 12:10-11

What are the implications of the Golden Rule in light of this passage?

The Word implies that when we treat others with consideration and respect that we are serving the Lord; how so?

Read Philippians 2:1-4

How does "doing nothing from selfishness or empty conceit" contribute to the unity of the Body of Christ?

Personal Application

Do rude and pushy people see the love and patience of Christ in me or do they see something else?

Is there someone in particular that I need to make an effort to be more gracious towards?

Where do I find the power to regard another as more important than myself?

Read Philippians 2:5-11

Chapter 5

DO NOT SPEAK AGAINST ONE ANOTHER

James warns us in 4:11, "Do not speak against one another, brethren. He, who speaks against a brother or judges his brother, speaks against the law and judges the law; but if you judge the law, you are not a doer of the law but a judge of it. There is only one Lawgiver and Judge, the One who is able to save and to destroy; but who are you who judge your neighbor."

The word that James uses for speak against one another in this passage means to slander someone or to speak negatively about someone when they cannot defend themselves. Our only speech to one another about one another ought to be edifying and uplifting. James tells us, "Do not speak against...do not slander...do not gossip about your brother or sister."

In Psalm 50, God says that gossip and slander are marks of the wicked. Listen to these words, "But to the wicked God says, 'You let your mouth loose in evil and your tongue frames deceit. You sit and speak against your brother; you slander your own mother's son'" (Ps. 50:16a, 19-20).

Psalm 101:5 records these words of the Lord. "Whoever secretly slanders his neighbor, him I will destroy; no one who has a haughty look and an arrogant heart will I endure." Do you hear the words of the Lord?

In Romans 1:30, the Apostle Paul wrote that haters of God can be identified by two things, "...gossip and slander." The very things that the Psalmist said identify the wicked.

In his second letter to the Corinthians, the Apostle Paul feared that he would find slander and gossip in their midst if he came to visit them.

We notice few sins which the Bible so roundly condemns as it does slander and gossip. These violate what James calls The Royal Law. He then identifies the Royal Law as this, "...You shall love your neighbor as you love yourself" (James 2:8).

When you speak about another when they are out of your presence, you should speak of them in the manner you would if they stood at your side, or to speak of them as you would wish them to speak of you when you are not present at their side.

The Bible condemns gossip and slander because they violate Christ's Royal Law. James then tells us that to speak against a brother is to speak against and to judge the Law of God. The right of judgment belongs to God; for He is the only one who can discern the deep things of the heart.

DO NOT COMPLAIN AGAINST ONE ANOTHER

It seems that this topic was heavy on his heart as James wrote his letter, for he brings it up again in James 5:9, "Do not complain, brethren, against one another, so that you yourselves may not be judged; behold, the Judge is standing right at the door."

The essence of this verse means that we should not blame one another for our troubles or our situations; that we not blame someone else for the place we presently stand. Such actions refer to murmuring of such things as, "Well, if you hadn't done this" or "If that pastor would just..." or "If that board of elders..." you blame someone else for the situation you are in, murmuring against them and holding a grudge against them.

The interesting thing about this passage is that James talks about the second coming of the Lord. He calls us to be patient as we await His return. We don't know when He is coming back, so be patient. He gives us the example of a farmer who plants his crop and then patiently waits for the harvest. While we patiently wait our Lord's return, let us not grumble or complain against one another. Why? Because He could appear at any time.

This admonition fits like a hand in a glove with John's call in 1 John 2:28, "Now, little children, abide in Him, so that when He appears, we may have confidence and not shrink away from Him in shame at His coming."

I believe that one reason the Lord does not let us know when his return will happen is because He understands human nature, and if we had that future date marked on the calendar, in our human nature we would tempt to let things slide up until the day before His return. Are you living as if He might appear at the end of this day? Do you live with that sense that the Judge is at the door? Both James and John call us to live in readiness.

Don't complain against one another; don't speak against one another, because the judge is at the door. He could appear, and you don't want to be found embarrassed and say, "Doggone it, I wish He could have waited a day or two." You want to be found ready.

DO NOT JUDGE ONE ANOTHER

Matthew 7:1-5 records these words of Jesus, "Do not judge so that you will not be judged. For in the way you judge, you will be judged; and by your standard of measure, it will be measured to you. Why do you look at the speck that is in your brother's eye, but do not notice the log that is in your own eye? Or how can you say to your brother, 'Let me take the speck out of your eye,' and behold the log is in your own eye? You hypocrite, first take the log out of you own eye, and then you will see clearly to take the speck out of your brother's eye."

Let's take a moment to stop and understand just what it is that Jesus is saying in this passage. The Greek word translated judge in this case has a deeper meaning than we normally give it. We use the word judge for a lot of things. It could be a judge sitting behind a bench before a courtroom. It can be a judge at a county fair who decides which steer he will place as the Grand Champion. It can be a judge at a baseball game, an umpire making the crucial calls. But the context in this passage means to set up oneself as judge, jury, and executioner; it means to condemn.

Jesus warns us not to condemn. He talks about making a judgment before we have all the facts in hand. We have a tendency to judge others by what we have heard, by what we perceive. And often our hearing and our perceiving are dead wrong.

The famous rabbi Hillel said, "Do not judge a man until you yourself have experienced his circumstances and his situation."

One snowy morning a businessman was walking down a city sidewalk that was slippery from an overnight snow. As he rounded a corner, he slipped, briefcase in hand; up he went, and down he fell in the gutter by the curb. He just so happened to fall beside a drunken man who had spent the whole night there; laying in his filth, empty bottle in hand. The businessman lay still for a moment, taking a mental inventory of any injuries he might have received in the fall.

In the meantime, people walked by, buses and taxis drove by, and what do the people see? They see two drunken men laying side by side in the gutter with an empty bottle lying between them. What do they conclude? These two have probably been up all night partying together. And who knows how many bottles they have consumed. We can only see the evidence of one, but we do see the evidence of a night of revelry and drunkenness.

Have the people walking by or riding in the taxi or the bus drawn a right conclusion about what they have just seen? No, they have not. One man lay there because he is a drunk. He laid there in his filth as a result of his pursuits of the previous night. The other man slipped and just as soon as he figures out that nothing is broken, he's going to pick himself up, dust himself off, pick up his briefcase, and go on to work.

I tell you this story so that I might now ask you, "How many times have you made such a judgment when you did not possess all the facts to make a righteous judgment?"

That is what Jesus speaks about. You are not the judge, the jury and the executioner. You be careful, for Jesus goes on to say that in the same way that you judge, you will be judged. If you show mercy, you will be shown mercy. If you are mean and nasty and judgmental, I guarantee you that it will come back to you one day in the same manner. You will howl as if you were jabbed with a red hot poker. You will reap only what you have sown by wrongly judging and speaking against another.

Listen to the words of Jesus found in John 7:24, "Do not judge according to appearance, but judge with righteous judgment."

Jesus is not telling us that within His Church and among those who follow His Word and His Law that there is not a place for righteous judgment. The Bible tells us that if someone in the body of Christ is living in blatant sin, it is to be dealt with. Because blatant, unrepentant sin in a church body can have the same affect that an unchecked cancerous tumor can have on a person's body. The Bible does not tell us to turn our heads the other way. There are times when God calls the church to apply discipline to the unruly and the unrepentant. (Matthew 18:15-17; 1 Corinthians 5:1-5).

When the Apostle Paul told us to speak the truth to one another in love, do you know what he meant? Speaking the truth to one another *is* love. Too many times in an effort to be kind and caring and loving, we end up sweeping things aside that we should confront and deal with. Because we don't deal with them they grow and fester and make a horrible mess somewhere down the road, a mess that could have been averted by the church simply obeying the words of Jesus. To love is to speak the truth.

Jesus said to make sure we have all the facts before we render judgment. Deal with one another in mercy, because in the way that you deal with another will be the manner in which you sooner or later will be dealt.

Romans 14:13 warns us, "Therefore, let us not judge one another anymore, but rather determine this, not to put an obstacle or a stumbling block in a brother's way."

The context of Romans 14 concerns matters of our conscience. It seems, from what we read and hear, that in some of the peripheral areas of the faith, individuals can hold differing opinions and neither one of them be wrong. In Romans 14:2, Paul says that one person has faith that he may eat all things, and another one eats vegetables only. Some people are vegetarians and some are not.

When I pastored in Southern Utah, one of my dear friends was a Seventh Day Adventist pastor. When we went out for breakfast, I never ordered bacon with my eggs. Why? Because that would have offended him. I have no problem eating bacon, and I'll come over to your house for ham or bacon or sausage any time. But he had a deep conviction about eating pork. So the last thing I would do would be to flaunt my liberty before a brother I love by throwing something offensive to him on the breakfast table that we shared. I could eat my bacon later. Paul calls us not to destroy fellowship over food.

Paul tells us that one person regards one day above another. And he asks, "Who are you to judge?"

At one time a woman attended the church I pastored who was raised in the old school of church etiquette. She believed with all her heart that when one goes to church they should wear their Sunday best. You would never have found her wearing slacks, blue jeans or shorts to church. But, she also did not stand in judgment over those who did not dress according to her convictions.

More than once in my 34 years of pastoral ministry, I have had to deal with what I call the "professional weaker brother," one who stumbled all the time, not because he was young in faith but because his standard for right and wrong was the standard of right and wrong for everyone in the church, or it had better be. These people live in perpetual judgment, and those around him are continually miserable. No grace, no mercy, all law, their law. That's why I call him the professional weaker brother. At times God calls us to curb our liberties before a brother or sister of weaker faith. But when a person has dwelt in the faith for 50 years, it's time to grow up.

Let me tell you a story.

During his senior year at Arizona State University, Pat Tillman was named the Pac10 Defensive Player of the year. In 1998 he was drafted by the Arizona Cardinals. Following the attacks on our nation on September 11, 2001, Pat Tillman turned down a $3.6 million contract with the Cardinals and joined the Army. After completing the Army ranger school, he was deployed to the Middle East as part of Operation Iraqi Freedom. And from there he was deployed to Afghanistan where on April 22, 2004, he was killed in action. The tragedy of Pat Tillman's death was he was killed by friendly fire. Pat Tillman was mortally wounded by one of his fellow rangers.

Why do I tell this story? Because as tragic as it is to say, the majority of those wounded in the body of Christ are wounded by their own, someone bent on being right, others bent on being first, yet others attempting to garner either attention or sympathy for themselves or inflict wounds on their fellow soldiers in Christ. The pride, the arrogance, the thoughtlessness that cause brothers and sisters in the faith to speak and complain against or judge one another, renders the body of Christ impotent and powerless.

Fastened to the front of our refrigerator for many years we had a small piece of paper with a quote from Phillip Yancey. Phillip asked this question, "What would it be like if when the world heard the word "Christian" that the first thing that came to their mind was love, joy, peace, patience, kindness, goodness, faithfulness, gentleness and self-control?"

Only one group of people have the capacity to make that happen in our community, and that's you, along with others committed to the Lord, and committed to one another, the fruit of the spirit flowing from our lives as we go.

I have no words to describe the pain that I feel in my heart when I hear Christians judging or speaking against one another. With God as my witness, like it is with my own children, I do not love one person more than another in the church that I serve. I would lay down my life for every one of them. It makes my blood run cold; it makes my heart ache, when I hear brothers and sisters speaking against another brother or sister. God has something better planned for us, as individuals and as a church.

I wish that we could covenant with one another today, to live together in a way that will build up the body and not tear down, that we could agree with one another today that we will not hear the gossip and the slander against another. And if someone does come to us with such words, that we would refuse to speak to them about that matter until they have personally gone to talk with the one that they want to talk about to us. Because, brothers and sisters, if we won't give in to gossip and slander and judgmentalism, it will die in our midst. It can die right where you stand by refusing to become part of it in the giving, by refusing to become part of it in the receiving.

Questions to Ponder

Read James 4:11

How would you define "speaking against" to a teenager?

In the context of James 4, the root cause of speaking against one another is pride. What is the cure for pride we find in James 4:6-10?

Read Psalm 101:5

What does the Psalmist suggest is the root cause of slander?

What is the cure?

Read John 7:24

While we are forbidden to judge or condemn another, John teaches that our judgments should be righteous. This may seem contradictory, but the word "righteous" simply refers to a life conditioned by God's standards.

What does John mean by righteous judgment?

When it comes to making righteous judgments, what is our written standard?

Has a negative story about you ever gotten back to you from another person?

How did you feel about it? What was the result?

Personal Application

Think about the last time you sinned by speaking against another. Is this a repetitive sin for you? What would God have you to do about it?

Think about the last time you held bitterness in your heart against another. What was the result? What should you have done in the first place?

If God were to grade you on "not judging" others today, would it be an A...B...C...D...F?

Why?

How can you make this issue right before God and right with others?

Chapter 6

ACCEPT ONE ANOTHER

The Apostle Paul sets Christ up as our example when he exhorts us to accept others. "Now we who are strong ought to bear the weaknesses of those without strength and not just please ourselves. Each of us is to please his neighbor for his good, to his edification. For even Christ did not please Himself; but as it is written, 'The reproaches of those who reproached You fell on Me.' For whatever was written in earlier times was written for our instruction, so that through perseverance and the encouragement of the Scriptures we might have hope. Now may the God who gives perseverance and encouragement grant you to be of the same mind with one another according to Christ Jesus, so that with one accord you may with one voice glorify the God and Father of our Lord Jesus Christ. Therefore, accept one another, just as Christ also accepted us to the glory of God" (Romans 15:1-7).

What does it mean to accept one another? The King James Version of the Bible gives us some help here. It says, "Receive one another just as Christ received us to the glory of God."

In this passage the Apostle Paul is coming to the end of his letter to the Church in Rome. In closing, he encourages them to bear one another's weaknesses, to strengthen one another, to live and work for the good of their neighbor, not just to please self.

When we deal with others in the Body of Christ we have to understand that we are individuals as different as night and day. In a recent prayer time, one brother mentioned the fact that if it were not for Jesus Christ, we would not be hanging out together.

We come together in fellowship because of the Lord Jesus Christ and the common salvation that we experience in Him. In fact, for some of us, He is the only thing we do have in common. Some of us have been Christians for many years; some of us are new to the faith. Some of us are just exploring the faith while some of us continue to search for the meaning of the gospel. We come from different denominational and cultural backgrounds.

For the past 34 years I have served the Lord by pastoring two community churches. I have survived because early on in my ministry I determined in my heart to lift up Christ, not denominational distinctiveness. The members of my present congregation come from many and varied expressions of the Christian faith, as well as converts who have never been part of a church before being saved. Week after week we gather together because of the One who has made us one, the Lord Jesus Christ.

The Apostle Paul said there exists but one body of Christ (Ephesians 4:4). Think about this. In Christ we have been made one. I know the world gets confused when they drive by a row of churches on some street, seeing them as different churches. But when God looks down on the worshiping millions across our land on a given Sunday, He sees one body, one church. When we determine in our hearts to walk together as one, in a visible way, we confirm the claims of the Lord Jesus Christ; the claim that He is the world's Messiah and Savior.

John 17 records for us a prayer that Christ offered up to His Father shortly before His crucifixion. Jesus prayed this prayer in the presence of His disciples somewhere outside of the gates of Jerusalem on the way to the Garden of Gethsemane. I read this prayer often because in it we hear and feel the heart of our Lord Jesus concerning those who follow Him.

Jesus prayed in John 17:11, "I am no longer in the world; and yet they themselves are in the world, and I come to You; Holy Father, keep them in Your name, the name which You have given Me, that they may be one even as we are."

Though He was with His disciples when He prayed this prayer, Jesus was also praying for you and me. "I do not ask on behalf of these alone, but for those also who believe in Me through their word; that they may all be one even as You, Father, are in Me and I in You, that they also may be in Us, so that the world may believe that you sent Me" (John 17:20-21).

Do you know who "they" are? It is us! Following Christ's Great Commission, the disciples went out and preached the gospel; people were saved. Those who were saved then shared the message with others, and so on, and so on, until the message reached you and me. And now, the Lord Jesus Christ calls us to continue sharing this message with others. Jesus was not praying only for the twelve but also for us, the ones who have come to believe because of *their* faithfulness. What is His prayer for us? That we may be one.

Jesus prayed further concerning unity. "The glory which You have given Me I have given to them, that they may be one, just as we are one; I in them and You in Me, that they may be perfected in unity, so that the world may know that You sent Me, and loved them, even as You have loved Me" (John 17:22-23).

I do not believe the church of the Lord Jesus Christ understands the true significance of these verses. In them we find the power to reveal Christ to a watching world.

Jesus has given to the world two standards of measure by which they may judge His Church. The first is unity. True unity in the Spirit gives evidence to a watching world that Jesus is who He claimed to be.

In John 13, Jesus spoke of further evidence that has the power to convince a watching world that we are truly His disciples. He said, "A new commandment I give to you, that you love one another, even as I have loved you, that you also love one another. By this will all men know that you are My disciples, if you have love for one another" (John 13:34-35).

Thus, the two things that have the most power to draw a watching world to the Savior are (1) unity in the church and (2) our visible love for one another. All too often, what is it a watching world sees in Christ's church? Division! Because brothers and sisters have refused to get on their knees together, get in the Word together, and pray together over their differences. If we would determine to walk together in unity and love, the watching world would be drawn to Jesus, just as He said it would be.

A watching and waiting world is filled with the same longings that we who are now Christians were born with: longings for meaning, significance, and love; longings that we can realize only in Jesus. As the body of Christ we have something to add to the power of Christ's testimony that they may see Him and believe. They will see Him when they see us accepting and receiving one another, and walking together as companions.

God calls us to walk together as companions, opening our arms, our lives and our homes to one another. This kind of walking together requires effort, patience, and understanding.

It takes effort to cultivate a friendship, doesn't it? I will never grow close to someone if I do not spend time with them.

How should we receive one another? Just as Christ received us and accepted us. Do you know what happens when we do this? God receives glory. Isn't that what we're living for?

Listen to these words from 1 Corinthians 10:31, "Whether, then, you eat or drink or whatever you do, do all to the glory of God."

We need to understand this. The chief purpose that God has given to us the gifts of life and breath and being is that we may proclaim the excellencies of Him who has brought us out of darkness into His marvelous light (1 Peter 2:9).

God did not create you for your own pleasure, but for His pleasure. When you live for the pleasure of God, guess what happens to your life? It becomes rich, fulfilling, and full of purpose. If you live for self, live for the moment – there will always be something lacking in your walk with Christ. When you eat and drink to the glory of God, and when you do everything you do to the glory of God, you will begin to experience what you were born and called to do, to live for Him.

When we accept one another with grace and mercy and love, it is an act of worship for it brings glory to Him.

SHOW TOLERANCE FOR ONE ANOTHER

Paul exhorts us in Ephesians 4:1-2, "Therefore I, the prisoner of the Lord, implore you to walk in a manner worthy of the calling with which you have been called, with all humility and gentleness, with patience, showing tolerance for one another in love."

The word "tolerance" has become a buzz word for the "politically correct" crowd of our day. We live in a day and age in which society asks us to tolerate one another and our differences. They want us to tolerate things which are evil and deviant in the sight of our Holy God. They ask us to tolerate things such as the gay lifestyle and to give our sanction to homosexual marriage. They want us to look the other way, tolerate it. God does not intend such an interpretation of this verse.

The King James word for tolerance is to "forebear." Do you know what forebear means? It means to endure or to put up with. And for what are we being asked? We are asked to put up with one another, to endure with one another in the Body of Christ.

We find this same thought in Colossians 3:12-13, "So, as those who have been chosen of God, holy and beloved, put on a heart of compassion, kindness, humility, gentleness and patience; bearing with one another, and forgiving each other, whoever has a complaint against anyone; just as the Lord forgave you, so also should you."

In the eyes of God we are holy and beloved through the cleansing of the blood that was shed by the Lord Jesus Christ. We are holy and beloved in the eyes of our Heavenly Father because of the completed work of Christ on the Cross. If that is true, we are then called to put on a heart of compassion, kindness, humility, gentleness, bearing with one another, or forbearing and tolerating one another ...just as the Lord does with you.

God does not call us to tolerate or put up with blatant sinful behaviors. The church is called to deal with sin in the camp. But that is not what this refers to here. Here, God is calling us to tolerate or put up with one another as we are growing together in Christ.

The Bible speaks of four stages of Christian growth: babes, children, young men, and fathers, stages of growth and maturation.

Every individual within the Body of Christ presently lives at one of these stages of growth, and is hopefully still growing.

Each of us dwells at a different stage of growth in Christ. Since we are all in a process, and since God is not finished with any of us yet, we are called to fore-bear with one another as we journey together. Those of you that may see yourself as young men or fathers, you at one time were babes, then you were a child, and you didn't get it right every time either.

Are you familiar with the things that real babies do? You are always wiping something off some part of their anatomy. And it's no different with baby Christians. Some days they get it right and some days they don't and when you get those babes in Christ potty trained, it is a wonderful day.

Little children don't learn everything at once. I know that when I was learning to ride a two wheeled bicycle, I experienced many bruised knees and scraped knuckles in the process. But with persever-ance came success.

We need to extend grace and mercy as we see different ones growing through their different predicaments and dilemmas, whatever God allows in their lives to shape them into His image. The call for tolerance springs from a realization that none of us dwell at the same place in our spiritual growth; we are all in process.

BE KIND TO ONE ANOTHER

The Apostle Paul wrote in Ephesians 4:32, "Be kind to one another, tender-hearted, forgiving each other, just as God in Christ also has forgiven you."

The Greek word for "kind" in this verse is *chrestos.* The Greeks identified this quality as the disposition of mind which thinks as much for its neighbor's good as it does for its own. Kindness has such a quality. Can you imagine what it would be like if this was played out in each of our lives?

The kind person is not preoccupied with self, but truly looks out for the good of those around him. This attitude epitomizes the attitude of our Savior who said that He came not to be served but to serve (Matthew

20:28). That's what kindness is. The kind person thinks more of another than oneself or before oneself.

BE OF THE SAME MIND TOWARD ONE ANOTHER

Romans 12:16 warns us, "Be of the same mind toward one another; do not be haughty in mind, but associate with the lowly. Do not be wise in your own estimation."

Then Romans 12:3, "For through the grace given to me I say to everyone among you not to think more highly of himself than he ought to think..."

I don't know if you have noticed it, but we live in a world that is continually establishing pecking orders. Do you know what a pecking order is? It's a farm term. On the farm, every flock of chickens has a pecking order. Do you know how the chickens arrive at that order? By which one can peck the hardest and the most in an effort to get the other chickens out of their way. When you go to feed a flock of chickens the ones at the top of the pecking order become the first ones to eat while the others shyly stand back and wait their turn. The animal kingdom thrives on establishing pecking orders; these are usually established by brute strength or intimidation.

We live in an age that establishes such orders by what you wear, the kind of car you drive, what subdivision you live in, how much money you make, or how many degrees you've earned. The scripture says that Christians are called to live a different way.

When we enter through the door of the church, pecking orders should die. We are one in Christ, servants of one another. And even when it comes to the appointed leaders in the church, true leadership is epitomized by a towel around the waist and a basin in the hand ready to wash the feet of everyone. The Bible calls us to humbly submit to one another. This is a choice to voluntarily rank ourselves under one another. How different from the way of the world.

James warns against showing favoritism, "My brethren, do not hold your faith in our glorious Lord Jesus Christ with an attitude of personal favoritism. For if a man comes into your assembly with a gold ring and dressed in fine clothes, and there also comes in a poor man in dirty clothes, and you pay special attention to the one who is wearing the fine clothes, and say, 'You sit here in a good place,' and you say to the poor man, 'You stand over there, or sit down by my footstool,' have you not made distinctions among yourselves, and become judges with evil motives? Listen, my beloved brethren: did not God choose the poor of this world to be rich in faith and heirs of the kingdom which He promised to those who love Him? But you have dishonored the poor man. Is it not the rich who oppress you and personally drag you into court? Do they not blaspheme the fair name by which you have been called?" (James 2:1-7).

One of my friends pastored a church which was attended by a United States Senator. He told me one day, "I could never let the Senator come to church without having to play the part of the big shot, especially for our visitors." He would say to the congregation, "Oh, it's so good to have the Senator with us today." The Senator pulled him aside and told him to knock it off.

The senator said, "When I come through this door, I am a brother in Christ. I'm here with my brothers and sisters, and I just want to melt into this family and worship my God, minister and be ministered unto. And if you don't knock it off, I will find another place to go to church."

All was well and good until the next time the Senator was in town. My friend told me, "I just couldn't keep my mouth shut. I had to let everybody know we had a Senator in our church." And staying true to his word that was the last time the Senator came to that church. He was just looking for a place to worship with his family in Christ.

When we enter through the doors of the church, we are to be of the same mind towards one another because in God's eyes there is no pecking order. The example set by His only begotten Son was to serve and not be served.

Romans 15:5-6, "Now may the God who gives perseverance and encouragement grant you to be of the same mind with one another according to Christ Jesus, so that with one accord you may with one voice glorify the God and Father of our Lord Jesus Christ."

This passage has a little different twist on it. Here God calls us to have the mind of Christ. And the Apostle exhorts us to be of the same mind with one another, because that is the mind of God towards us.

In his letter to the Philippians, the Apostle Paul exhorts us to have this attitude, for this was the mind that was in Christ Jesus (Phil. 2:5).

God Himself extends perseverance and encourage-ment towards us so that we may extend the same to one another.

Matthew Henry, Puritan minister and Bible expositor, wrote a commentary of the Old and New Testaments between the years 1708 and 1710. In light of the verses that we have explored in this chapter listen to the words of this man. "Patience implies a bearing in-jury without seeking revenge. To forebear with another in love signifies tolerating another's weaknesses or shortcomings out of a principle of love. And so as not to cease loving on account of these. Christians need to bear with one another, and to make the best of one an-other, provoking one another to love and good deeds. Without these things, unity cannot be preserved."[1]

Questions to Ponder

Read John 17:20-23

How does unity in the church bear witness to a watching world that Christ is who He claimed to be? Have you personally experienced a bit of what Jesus is praying for? What was that like?

Have you experienced the opposite? What was that like?

Do you have some ideas how your church can continue on welcoming/accepting one another in the fellowship?

Read Ephesians 4:1-3 and Colossians 3:12-13

The Bible tells us that there are four stages of Christian growth, babes, children, young men, and fathers. How might keeping this in mind help us to show tolerance for one another?

Forbearing with one another must accompany proper equipping for growth. Are you growing and maturing in Christ?

Read Romans 12:16 and James 2:1-4

In nine separate passages, the Bible tells us that God is no respecter of persons and does not show partiality. What can we do to resist making distinctions such as the world makes among ourselves as Christians?

Personal Application

Ask God to help you identify ways that you can better show your acceptance of others.

Look for opportunities to display kindness to another.

Ask God to identify areas of intolerance in your life and for a greater grace to tolerate those who you see as different than you.

Chapter 7

EDIFY ONE ANOTHER

—ᨆᨆ—

One of my favorite passages of scripture is in the third chapter of Colossians. The interesting thing about the third chapter of Colossians is that it shows us that Christian growth does not happen by osmosis. To grow in Christ demands something of us.

The Apostle Paul wrote, "So as those who have been chosen of God, holy and beloved, put on a heart of compassion, kindness, humility, gentleness and patience; bearing with one another, and forgiving each other, whoever has a complaint against anyone; just as the Lord forgave you, so also should you. Beyond all these things put on love, which is the perfect bond of unity. Let the peace of Christ rule in your hearts, to which indeed you were called in one body; and be thankful. Let the word of Christ richly dwell within you, with all wisdom teaching and admonishing one another with psalms and hymns and spiritual songs, singing with thankfulness in your hearts to God. Whatever you do in word or deed, do all in the name of the Lord Jesus, giving thanks through Him to God the Father" (Colossians 3:12-17).

This passage is full of things that God calls us to do. It is full of action words such as "put on."

We can understand such words because we have all put on something today. God calls us to put on compassion, kindness, humility, gentleness, and patience just as we would put on our shirt, our dress, or our shoes.

In verse fifteen the apostle tells us that there are some things we must allow to happen to us. He says, "Let the peace of Christ rule in your hearts." I used to think that if the peace of Christ did not reign in my heart that it was someone else's fault. But the word "let" shows me that I have a choice in the matter.

Today, if the peace of Christ does not reign in your heart, it's because you, in some way, have refused to let it reign in your heart. You have to make a choice to let the peace of Christ reign in your heart. It's your choice. It's something you do.

Verse sixteen tells us to let the word of Christ richly dwell in us. For that to happen you have to bring yourself to the word and bring the word into yourself.

Then in verse seventeen the apostle says, "Whatever you do in word or deed, do all in the name of the Lord Jesus."

Those are great words: put on, bear with, forgive, let, and be thankful, whatever you do. There is nothing passive about growing as a Christian. Christian growth is filled with deliberate acts that cause us to grow closer to Christ and to one another.

TEACH ONE ANOTHER

In Colossians 3:16, the Apostle Paul exhorts us with these words, "Let the word of Christ richly dwell within you, with all wisdom teaching and admonishing one another with psalms and hymns and spiritual songs, singing with thankfulness in your hearts to God."

As a Christian, whether you know it or not, whether you believe it or not, God has called you to be a teacher in some form or fashion. In this passage, Paul exhorts us to teach one another. This speaks to the members of the body of Christ. It does not speak specifically to those with a teaching or preaching gift. Rather, it talks to all of us. Teach one another. This passage refers to the holding of discourse with others in order to instruct them, to impart an instruction, to instill a doctrine to explain a thing. In your personal study of God's word, you do not just fill your head with knowledge; but you come to know Christ in such a way that you might share Him with others.

When you study God's Word, do you just look for interesting facts, or do you look for your Lord? Remember what Jesus said about the scriptures, "It is these that bear witness of me." Do you look for Him when you open those precious pages? Do you see yourself as sitting down before Him and hearing His words of life?

One thing that delights my heart is to visit with a brother or a sister, and to hear them share what God is doing in their life, what they sense that God is speaking to them, and how He is leading them. I love to talk with people about Jesus and what they sense He is doing in their life.

I want to ask you a question. What have you discovered of God this past week that you did not know last week? Think about this, in this past week what new thing, what fresh thing has God revealed to you as you have spent time in His presence? It's brand new, it's fresh, and it's exciting. Now I ask you, with who have you shared it?

I know how people act when they have purchased a new car. They drive it around and show it to family members and to friends. They are so excited that they have to share that excitement with someone.

It's alright to get excited about such things, but do you get as excited about the fresh things that Christ speaks to your heart day by day? Are you as anxious to share those things with your family and friends, as excited as you are to tell them about your latest vacation or your newest toy?

When God shares something new with you, don't hold it in. Share it with someone. Become a teacher of the things that He shares with you.

ADMONISH ONE ANOTHER

Colossians 3:16 also calls us to admonish one another. Consider Romans 15:14, "And concerning you, my brethren, I myself also am convinced that you yourselves are full of goodness, filled with all knowledge, and able also to admonish one another."

The Apostle Paul, in this verse, speaks to the body of Christ. He is saying that because God's goodness dwells in us, because His knowledge is growing in us, we are able to admonish one another rightly.

The word "admonish" means to caution or to reprove gently. This stands as one of the duties of members of the body of Christ for which I am personally thankful.

I have often commented on the fact that I need the Body of Christ to tell me when my "spiritual slip" is showing. Allow me to expand on that thought. When I was growing up, in a family of sisters, and at the time I was growing up, the girls could not wear slacks or pants to school – they wore dresses. I can remember my sisters coming into the living room before school or church and make a little pirouette and ask, "Is my slip showing?"

The problem was that they could not see it because the hem of their skirt or dress hid the slip from their view. According to the response of the person they were asking, they would make the necessary adjustments to the slip.

Because sometimes my spiritual slip shows, I need my brothers and sisters in Christ who will lovingly make me aware of that fact. None of us has arrived yet, and all of us have a limited peripheral vision. Some things about myself I cannot see; I have spiritual blind spots.

God, in His grace, and in His mercy, and because He loves us so much, has provided us with brothers and sisters in Christ to speak into our lives, to gently caution us when our spiritual slip shows. What do I mean by that? When something arises out of our lives inconsistent with our claim to be a Christian, we need someone who loves us and cares for us to speak into our lives.

God has saved me from myself. God has saved the church that I pastor, through the admonishing words of brothers and sisters in Christ, who have come to me prayerfully, carefully, and even trembling, saying, "Pastor, I don't know if you see it, but..." And you know what? When such a word has come by someone who loves me and was truly seeking God's direction, a funny thing happens. The Holy Spirit usually beat them to my door step. And when they came through the door, I already knew why they were there. When they brought a word, it was a confirming word, and my heart was already broken and I was already seeking the Lord's forgiveness and restitution.

I need that in my life, and you need that in your life, because there are parts and places in your life you cannot see, that only others can see. I would ask you to think about this. Who has permission to speak into your life in this way? Who has permission to speak the things you need to hear without the hair on your neck standing up and your defenses coming up? Who has that permission in your life?

We all need three types of people in our lives. We need a Paul, we need a Timothy, and we need a Barnabas. A Paul, is someone who speaks into our life as a mentor. A Timothy, is someone whose life we speak into as a mentor. A Barnabas, is someone who loves us but is not impressed with us and will speak God's truth into our lives and encourage us to greater heights and depths in God.

If and when God calls us to speak an admonishing word to another, we better first go to our knees before God, because when we come with words of admonishment to someone, we do not swoop in on them from a higher plane to show them the error of their way. Rather, we come to them on our knees, humbling ourselves, appealing to them, from the very heart of the living God.

I know of examples where a brother or a sister has gone to another with an admonishing word that did not come from the Lord. Therefore, when they went to this brother or sister and said what they had to say, it wounded and destroyed the one to whom they spoke. They tore the guts out of their brother or sister; they ripped their heart out, and then stomped on it.

When the spirit of God leads a person to speak an admonishing word, it will be a word spoken in God's timing and in God's way. It will not be your words but God's words speaking through you.

I know this is a tough lesson because we have to come to trust one another for this to happen. We have to build relationships with one another. This does not happen when we avoid one another. This is one reason why small groups are risky. You meet with somebody every week for awhile and you know what? The stuff that you may smuggle in and out of church every Sunday is likely to be discerned in the smaller group. If we allow it, intimacy with one another grows in the small group. The masks come off and we begin to share our true selves, walls come down, transparency emerges, God begins to do something real and deep in our lives, making us one as He would have us to be.

I thank God for the brothers and sisters in Christ that He has sent my way over the years to speak His correction into my life. Many have been the times when something was hiding in my spiritual blind spots, things that I could not see. When these members of my family in Christ came, they came in love and in humility; they came broken and they spoke from God.

Proverbs 27:6 says, "Faithful are the wounds of a friend..."

I ask you again, who has the permission in your life to speak to you in such a way?

SPEAK TO ONE ANOTHER IN PSALMS, HYMNS AND SPIRITUAL SONGS

"Therefore be careful how you walk, not as unwise men but as wise, making the most of your time, because the days are evil. So then do not be foolish, but understand what the will of the Lord is. And do not get drunk with wine, for that is dissipation, but be filled with the Spirit, speaking to one another in psalms and hymns and spiritual songs, singing and making melody with your heart to the Lord; always giving thanks for all things in the name of our Lord Jesus Christ to God, even the Father; and be subject to one another in the fear of Christ" (Ephesians 5:15).

Let me share something with you that is my own personal opinion. Because it is my own personal opinion, you can take it or leave it. The Apostle Paul, when he wrote the seventh chapter of First Corinthians, says that what he had to say about a certain matter came from the Lord, but his advice on another matter was his personal opinion. I find that statement incredible! He literally says, "You don't have to do what I say here because this is my personal opinion." But another place he says pay attention because this is the heart of God.

I want to share something with you about music, about song. I believe with all my heart that song is unique to the human race. I believe that the ability to sing is a gift that God gave to the human race alone, a gift that man would use to offer up praise, adoration and worship to his God.

In song, God has gifted us to collect our thoughts and lift with our vocal chords, hymns and songs of praise unto God. At this point someone may say, "But the angels sing." We can find no place in the Bible that says angels sing, and if your Bible says they do then it is because you have a modern translation Bible that has altered the original languages.

On the night the angels appeared to the shepherds outside of Bethlehem, to announce to shepherds the birth of the Messiah, the Bible says that the angel was joined by a multitude of heavenly hosts, "Praising God and saying, 'Glory to God in the highest, peace and goodwill toward men'" (Luke 2:13-14).

In the sixth chapter of Isaiah, the seraphim are flying around the throne of God, calling out to one another, "Holy, holy, holy, is the Lord of Hosts." We can find no evidence in the whole Bible stating that angels sing. I don't believe they do! I believe that the gift of song is unique to mankind. It was ultimately given to him that he might raise with the instrument of his vocal chords, praises and high praises of worship unto his God.

In Genesis 4:21, you will read about a man named Jubal. Jubal created the first musical instrument, and from his name we derive the words jubilation and jubilee, celebrations in song.

When you look up the definitions of the words in Ephesians and Colossians, "psalms and hymns and spiritual songs" – every one of them is a musical expression. Something in us makes us want to sing, whether we can carry a tune or not. We sing in the shower, in the car, wherever we are.

The Psalms exhort us to sing a new song unto the Lord (Ps. 96:1). Do you know what that means? It literally means to sing a new and unpremeditated chant unto the Lord. It is a song that has not been written down. It is a song that rises up from your innermost being, a fresh chant of praise unto the Lord that wells up from the depths of your heart as you raise your hands and voice unto the Lord in spontaneous praise and worship. How is this expressed? In psalms, hymns and in spiritual songs. We are exhorted by the word to sing to the Lord our God. We can do it alone. We are called to do it with one another.

One of the greatest witnesses of the Christian faith is the music it has produced. If I had my way, every member of the church I pastor would be required to take a course in hymnody. Hymnody is the study of the music of the church. We have a rich heritage and even the world loves our music. I dare say that when we go to hear a production of Handel's Messiah at Christmas time, Christians are probably a minority in the performance hall. But when the choir begins to sing that great Hallelujah Chorus, what does everyone in the room do? They stand! There's something about it that moves us, and it moves us deeply.

In the Protestant church, the focal point of corporate worship is the preaching of the word. In the Roman Church, the focal point is the mass and the Eucharist. But in the Protestant Church the preaching of the Word has always been preceded by singing. When we sing the praises of our Lord, that singing centers our thoughts on God, it prepares our hearts to receive the word of God.

When we go to church on Sunday morning, most of us come from a busy and crazy week. We come contemplating the busy and crazy week that lies out before us. But when we gather together and sing the high praises of our God, when we begin to focus on God, as one song writer put it, "The things of earth grow strangely dim in the light of His glory and grace." Then, all of a sudden, our hearts are prepared, through the singing of these psalms, and hymns and spiritual songs – prepared to receive the Word of God as seeds implanted in our hearts. Yes, the singing unto God primes the pump, tills the soil of our hearts to hear the Word of God.

I have been saddened and heartbroken over the years by the battles over music in the Church. Churches have been split by "worship wars," battles over styles of music to be used in the worship service.

One noted pastor of our day has said that there is no such thing as Christian music, just Christian lyrics. He is right. I could play a song for you that is just a melody and you would be hard pressed to tell me if it was Christian or not. Only by hearing the words could you tell whether the song was secular or sacred.

Recently someone asked me, after we had sung the old hymn "Morning Has Broken" in a Sunday worship service, "Why did we sing a Cat Stephens song this morning?" Well, because Cat Stevens did not write that song, a Christian did. The song is a song written unto our Creator and Lord. Cat Stevens merely chose to record it at some point in his career.

Though Judy Collins, in my humble opinion, sang Amazing Grace as none other has ever sang it, she did not write it. It was written by a former slave trader named John Newton, who upon coming to faith in Christ realized the expanse of God's Amazing Grace.

We live in a world of many styles of music, and, contrary to popular belief, they all can be used to praise the Lord. God isn't interested in the notes, or the beat. He is interested in the heart of those who come to worship. The truth is we can come to church on Sunday morning and sing for a half an hour and never have worshiped. On the other hand, when the attitude of the heart is right, it's possible to sing one song and be ushered into the presence of the Lord.

I am so thankful that God has given us the gift of song. His unique gift to mankind was a gift to be used first and foremost, to worship Him. God calls us to worship Him in song, to worship with one another. He calls us to teach, admonish, and encourage one another through song. Moreover, God calls us to be a singing people. When we get to heaven we will be a singing people.

One day Cliff Barrows told Billy Graham, "When we get to heaven, you're going to be out of a job. We musicians are going to have work to do. For, there is no mention of any preaching in heaven, but there is mention of singing."

SPEAK TRUTH TO ONE ANOTHER

"Do not lie to one another, since you laid aside the old self with its evil practices, and have put on the new self who is being renewed to a true knowledge according to the image of the one who created him..." (Colossians 3:9-10).

Do not lie to one another is the same as saying, "Speak truth to one another." Why does God call us to be truthful and honest with one another? Because we have lain aside that old lying and deceitful part of us and are being renewed every day into the image of Christ. Christ is all about truth. Isn't that right? Christ is all about truth!

The Book of Proverbs has much to say about this matter. Let us look at a few examples.

"For my mouth will utter truth; and wickedness is an abomination to my heart" (Proverbs 8:7).

"He who speaks truth tells what is right, but a false witness, deceit" (Proverbs 12:17).

"Truthful lips will be established forever, but a lying tongue is only for a moment" (Proverbs 12:19).

And again, "Lying lips are an abomination to the Lord, but those who deal faithfully are His delight" (Proverbs 12:22).

We live in a world of lies and half truths. Many stretch the truth or cut the truth in half to say whatever they want to say. And sadly it is not just the world outside our door. As Christian students, when taking a test, being a person of truth means we do not cheat. As Christians when filing our income taxes, it means we are honest and we declare all of our income. That's being a person of truth. A Christian businessperson does not cut the corners to get around government regulations that they personally do not like or agree with.

Every three months when I send in my quarterly income tax estimated payments, as I am writing the check, I praise God, because He has supplied not only the resources to put a roof over my head, clothes on my body, and food for my family, but he knows I need to make that check out too, and He furnishes that as well. I can say thank you, Lord. As a Christian, I don't have to cut ethical corners and neither do you. We are called to be a people of truth, a people of honesty and integrity in our speaking and in our doing, and in our being. The world outside of our door operates by a different rule, but we are called to live by God's.

It starts in our local church by being honest with one another. We are the ones that should tell the truth, the whole truth, and nothing but the truth to the glory of God. Even when it hurts, telling the truth is always the best option. Even a white lie is black in God's book.

Nothing undermines personal relationships like being lied to. I'd rather have somebody steal from me, slap me, spit in my face – than lie to me. Lying does something down inside of us. When you've been lied to, you wonder if you can ever trust what that person says again. Do you know what I'm talking about?

I pray that we would be a people of truth, a people who speak the truth to one another in love, a transparent and a humble people as we journey side by side with one another. What God desires for us cannot happen if we are not honest with one another or if we are not transparent with one another.

What was the first thing that Adam and Eve did when they sinned? They hid. And we have been hiding from each other ever since. If there is one arena in the whole world where we ought to be free to come out of hiding, it should be in the presence of our Christian family. God calls us to tolerate one another and not talk against one another, because we are all in the process of growing into Christ-likeness. God has not yet finished perfecting us. So He calls us to extend grace and tolerance to one another. We need to be open faced, transparent and honest with one another.

In the family of God we are called to live with one another in such a way that the world around us will catch a whiff of the fragrance of Jesus as they witness not only the testimony of our lives together but also the integrity of our lives in our day to day dealings in the world. There ought to be a noticeable difference since we are people of truth.

A few years ago I had a husband and wife in my office that had just filled out the paper work for a home loan. They had falsified their financial statement because they were afraid if they disclosed a certain amount of indebtedness, they would not get the loan. And you know what? The Holy Spirit wouldn't even let them drive home in peace. They could not even look one another in the face because of the guilt they felt. In the process they drove from the realtor's office to mine. They came into my office and confessed what they had just done. They then asked me, "What should we do?" I asked, "What do you think you should do?

They answered, "We need to return to the realtor's office and disclose the right numbers."

They also added, "But it may cost us the loan."

I said, "Well, that's the risk you're going to have to take."

After we had prayed together, they left my office and went back to the realtor's office and changed the numbers. In the end, they still got the loan, but in the meantime they had a clear conscience and could once again look one another in the face.

God's children don't have to manipulate the truth. Let us be a people of honesty and integrity, first to one another, and then in our dealings with the world outside our door, that the world may see Him and sense Him when we pass through their lives.

Question to Ponder

Read Colossians 3:16 and Romans 15:14

This passage calls us to admonish one another. What is necessary for someone to have permission to speak to us in such a manner?

What is the risk when we do not have such a person in our life?

Describe what happened in your life when another took time to either teach or admonish you?

What might be the lasting fruit of consistent teaching and admonishing among believers?

Read Psalm 51:6

Where must truth ultimately reside if we are going to be a people who speak truth to one another?

Read Ephesians 4:15

What does speaking the truth to one another in love mean?

The first place many of us fail to speak the truth to one another is when someone greets us with a, "How are you?" What keeps us from speaking the truth in these moments?

Read Ephesians 5:15-20

Identify the actions that prepare us for speaking to one another in psalms, hymns, and spiritual songs?

Personal Application

What has God shown you recently that is new and fresh to you? Have you shared it with another?

What keeps you from sharing with another your personal struggles, needs, failures, or disappointments?

Chapter 8

ENCOURAGE ONE ANOTHER

Paul wrote, "Therefore encourage one another and build up one another, just as you also are doing" (1 Thessalonians 5:11).

The call to encourage one another is a call to come alongside one another to exhort and build up one another. The Greek word for encourage in this passage is the word *paracletos*. Have you heard the word *paracletos* before? Jesus used it when referring to the ministry of the Holy Spirit, the Helper that He mentioned in His last discourse with His disciples found in John 13-16.

Jesus said that He must go away so that the Helper may come. And the Helper was the *paracletos* of God, the Holy Spirit, the one who comes alongside to help, to assist, to teach, to encourage, and to guide us. In this manner, God has called us to do to one another what the Holy Spirit does for us. We are to come alongside of one another, to walk, exhort, encourage, and to bring consolation to one another. "But encourage one another day after day as long as it is still called 'Today,'..." (Hebrews 3:13).

Do you know what procrastination is? It means putting off until tomorrow the thing that you could do or should do today. As a boy I used to try that on my mother, "Mom, isn't it true that we are not supposed to put off until tomorrow that which can be done today? Of course she would answer, "Yes." Then I would respond, "Can I have that last piece of chocolate cake?"

We can apply this same thought in many different ways. In this verse, the Apostle Paul calls us to encourage one another, day after day, as long as it is still called today. I believe the scripture tells us to have our eyes open as we mingle, walk, share and care for one another. God would have our eyes open so that we might discern the times and ways that we may speak a word of encouragement, of consolation and exhortation into the lives of our brothers and sisters in Christ.

Hebrews 10:25 speaks to us the same thing, "...but encourage one another; and all the more as you see the day drawing near."

As Christians, one of our duties is to encourage people. Do you know any "wet blanket" type people?

They are always ready to rain on someone's parade. We see our world full of them. They whine and complain; every bad thing in their lives is the fault of another. God wants us to be a people of encouragement.

Recently, as we saw gasoline prices climb, I asked a person who was sinking into discouragement, "Who is your source?" Their answer to me was, "God is my source." So I reminded them that God knows exactly how much gas they need to get to work and back, and to do the things they legitimately need to do.

What does God's Word tell us? "Seek first the kingdom of God and His righteousness and all of these things will be added unto you" (Matthew 6:33). So, if the believer endeavors to practice this command, guess what God will do? He will supply all of the gasoline we need on a daily basis. And while the world is discouraged and frustrated and wringing its hands, we Christians can stand out in the world by becoming people of encouragement. Why? Because our trust isn't in the oil companies. Our trust is in our Lord Jesus Christ who has promised to meet all of our needs according to His riches. Therefore, my brothers and sisters, we can afford to be the most encouraging people that walk the face of the earth.

Romans 12:2 exhorts the believer by saying, "...do not be conformed to this world, but be transformed..." Literally this passage tells us: do not let the world squeeze you into its mold. It will take a fight with our flesh to avoid contamination by the discouragements of this world. God wants us to become encouragers.

In the Acts of the Apostles we read of a man named Barnabas, whose very name meant "son of encouragement." Barnabas was the champion of the underdog. When Paul was the underdog, Barnabas stood by him (Acts 9:27). He was on hand for John Mark when he was the underdog (Acts 15:36-39). Furthermore, he supported the church in Jerusalem, helping the poor and the needy by selling a piece of property and laying the proceeds at the apostles' feet (Acts 4:36-37). When you study the life of Barnabas, his life excels as a character study in encouragement.

BUILD UP ONE ANOTHER

"...and build up one another..." (1 Thessalonians 5:11). Paul calls us by the Word of God to build up one another. I want to address this command from two different angles from a literal meaning and also a metaphorical meaning. Literally, to build up is to build a house or erect a building. How interesting to watch the progress on a new house. The builders clear the land, dig the trenches, lay the foundation, build the floors, erect the walls, shingle the roof, and transform the inside with windows, sheetrock, carpet and paint, until the house is ready for a family to move in.

In regards to the one another admonitions, the first recipients should be our families. If God has started to work the truths of the one another admonitions into your life, the first ones to whom it should be obvious is your family. Are you building them up? Are you encouraging them?

As a father, at times it seemed easier for me to see the one thing my children did wrong rather than the 99 things they did right. They needed my encouraging words for the 99.

Listen to these words:

They say the world is round, and yet

I think it's often square.

So many little hurts we get

From corners here and there.

But there is one truth that I have found

While journeying east and west.

The only folks we really wound

Are those we love the best.

We flatter those we scarcely know,

We please a fleeting guest,

And deal many a thoughtless blow

To those we claim to love the best.[1]

Being and doing to one another starts at home for each of us. Proverbs speaks much about building up and tearing down. And the main tool for both is the words of our mouth. With a word we can make a person wish they had never been born. Yet with a word we can make them soar on eagle's wings. Let's build up one another. Let's begin at home.

Metaphorically speaking, to build up means to promote Christian growth in wisdom, affection, grace, virtue, and holiness. The Lord calls us to come alongside of one another and to encourage one another as we grow together in the faith.

COMFORT ONE ANOTHER

"Therefore comfort one another with these words" (1 Thessalonians 4:18).

We must remember that context is king when we study the scriptures. Therefore we must understand the context of this passage. If you will read chapter four in its entirety, you will notice the last verse begins with the word "therefore." Every time we come to the word "therefore" we need to stop and ask the question, "What's it therefore?"

Chapter four of I Thessalonians refers to the second coming of Jesus. It talks about the hope of resurrection life. In the context of this passage, Paul speaks about the hope of the second coming of Jesus, the hope we have of life beyond the grave. The early church truly believed that they would be the generation that would witness the return of Christ. We need to understand that fact.

According to scripture, the last days is that interim of time between Jesus' ascension into heaven and His second coming. We have been living in the last days for the past 2000 years. Paul, Peter and John talked much about the last days. We are in the last days! How do we know we're in the last days? John answered that question by saying, "Because the anti-Christ is among us" (I John 3:18).

The Apostles Paul, Peter, and John believed that they would be the generation that saw the second coming of the Lord Jesus. So you know what they did? They encouraged one another. You know why they needed to encourage one another? Because they suffered for the name of the Lord Jesus. They suffered the loss of position, and possession; they were tortured, imprisoned, and lost family members. The belief of hope beyond this life, and life beyond the grave, the belief that the Lord Jesus would come one day and set all things right, not only gave them great comfort in their tribulations, it stirred a hope within them with which they comforted one another.

Here's how that hope works. One day, evil will have run its course. And then righteousness will reign forever and ever; comfort one another with these words. Comfort one another with these words because in the world yet to come, the aches and pains, the tears will vanish. Jesus is coming again. If the early church comforted one another with words of the second coming of Christ, as those who are 2000 years closer to that date than they were, how much more ought we to encourage one another? He's coming again!

Paul also spoke of another kind of comfort. This comfort I mention at every funeral I perform. Second Corinthians 1:3-4 says, "Blessed be the God and Father of our Lord Jesus Christ, the Father of mercies and the God of all comfort, who comforts us in all our affliction so that we will be able to comfort those who are in any affliction with the comfort with which we ourselves are comforted by God."

Have you ever gone through a deep, dark valley of your own where you felt the Lord's presence and you found His comfort sweet? And in a matter of time you were able to use the comfort that you received to comfort another going through a like valley, predicament, trial, or tribulation.

God is the God of all comfort. So if we can find any true comfort in the world, guess where it comes from? It comes from God. If He is the God of all comfort, then in one way or another, all comfort originates from Him. Paul said that when you walk through your personal valleys, trials, tribulations, and testing, and in them you find the beautiful and wonderful comfort of God, pass it on. Comfort one another with the comfort you received from God. Point those around you who suffer to the comforter that you found. The Lord calls us to comfort one another, with the wonderful truth that evil one day will come to an end and righteousness will prevail. One day Jesus will return to set up His kingdom of peace, joy and love. Comfort one another with these words.

CARE FOR ONE ANOTHER

Listen to these words concerning the Body of Christ? "For the body is not one member, but many. If the foot says, 'Because I am not a hand, I am not part of the body,' it is not for this reason any the less a part of the body. And if the ear says, 'Because I am not an eye, I am not part of the body,' it is not for this reason any the less a part of the body. If the whole body were an eye, where would the hearing be? If the whole body were hearing, where would the sense of smell be? But now God has placed the members, each one of them, in the body just as He desired. If they were all one member where would the body be? But now there are many members, but one body. And the eye cannot say to the hand, 'I have no need of you'; or again the head to the feet, 'I have no need of you.' On the contrary, it is much truer that the members of the body which seem to be weaker are necessary; and those members of the body which we deem less honorable, on these we bestow more abundant honor; and our less presentable members become more presentable, whereas our more presentable members have no need of it. But God has so composed the body, giving more abundant honor to that member which lacked, so that there may be no division in the body, but that these members may have the same care for one another. And if one member suffers, all the members suffer with it; if one member is honored, all the members rejoice with it" (1 Corinthians 12:14-26).

Here the Apostle Paul compares the Body of Christ to a person's physical body. How is our physical body composed? We have a skeleton to which tendons and muscles are attached that enable us to walk and grasp and lift and hug. Within our bodies God has placed various organs that work in concert to keep us alive and healthy. In our chest we have a heart that pumps blood through miles of arteries, veins, and capillaries. We possess two lungs that keep that blood supplied with life-giving oxygen. All of these individual parts are necessary for survival.

Paul also tells us that if Christ's body is to be alive and healthy, each and every member of the Body of

Christ is vital, each member so entwined with one another, so caring for one another, that when one weeps, we all weep with them. And when one rejoices, we all shout hallelujah together. Why? Because if one member of the body is in pain, the whole body feels that pain. And if one member dances in joy, the whole body has a reason to dance. To care for one another means to be mindful of another's needs, as well as willing to provide the necessary care.

James 2:14-17 says, "What use is it, my brethren, if someone says he has faith but he has no works? Can that faith save him? If a brother or sister is without clothing and in need of daily food, and one of you says to them, 'Go in peace, be warmed and be filled,' and yet you do not give them what is necessary for their body, what use is that? Even so faith, if it has no works, is dead, being by itself."

To do what these verses say means that we must open ourselves up to the power of God that gives us the capacity to truly regard one another as more important than ourselves. It means giving God permission to interrupt our busy lives so that we may sense and hear the cries of those around us and then willingly move in their direction to render aid and comfort. Someone has said, "You cannot do a kindness too soon because you never know how soon it will be too late."

SERVE ONE ANOTHER

Galatians 5:13, "For you were called for freedom, brethren; only do not turn your freedom into an opportunity for the flesh, but through love serve one another."

The word servant comes from the Greek word *dulos*, which literally means a slave. Now before you take this in a bad or negative context, note this is the word Paul used when he proclaimed that he was a bond servant of the Lord Jesus Christ. He said I am a bond servant, and Jesus is my master. Paul was indeed Christ's slave, but a slave who was motivated by love. He was a willing slave who surrendered his life to Christ with joy.

Jesus told his disciples, "You know that the rulers of the Gentiles lord it over them, and their great men exercise authority over them. It is not this way among you, but whoever wishes to become great among you shall be your servant, and whoever wishes to be first among you shall be your slave; just as the Son of Man did not come to be served, but to serve, and to give his life as a ransom for many" (Matthew 20:20-28).

What does Jesus say? If you wish to be great in my kingdom you must become a servant to others.

Then what did Jesus do? He set Himself before them as the example that they are to follow. Jesus, the Creator of the universe, has come among them as a servant Himself, coming to serve and not to be served. Anytime you have doubts about what our posture towards one another is to be, look to Jesus, the greatest servant of all.

I believe that many Christians never experience the deep joy that our faith has to offer because the joy of Christianity is enhanced and multiplied through service to one another.

In John 4, we read of Jesus and His disciples traveling through the region of Samaria. Jesus is hot, tired and thirsty so he sat down beside a well dug many centuries before by the great Hebrew patriarch Jacob. As he sat by the well his disciples went to a nearby village to buy some food. While they are gone Jesus made the acquaintance of and began to talk to a Samaritan woman who has come to draw water from the well.

When the disciples returned and tried to get Jesus to eat, He, in effect, told them that He was not hungry. They began to question among themselves if someone else had brought Him something to eat. He told them that He had food to eat that they know not of.

Do you know what food revived him? Doing the work of His Father. He said, "My meat is to do the will of Him who sent me."

God, the Father, imparts vitality to the life of the believer when the believer begins to look beyond his own needs and begins to serve others; a supernatural vitality that permeates into the body and soul. Do you know of this vitality?

Brothers and sisters, I know that sometimes service looks too much like work, but let me tell you something: the greatest joy in the kingdom of God is serving one another. It stands as the fountainhead of great and lasting joy. It means entering into the very existence of Christ and what He did when He walked among us as He came to be a servant to us all.

SHOW HOSPITALITY TO ONE ANOTHER

First Peter 4:9 exhorts us, "Be hospitable to one another without complaint." The Bible talks about hospitality in a couple different places, and interestingly it is different in each instance. In this passage, hospitality speaks of a person who is generous to guests, who opens up their arms as well as their home. We need to extend great hospitality to our brothers and sisters in Christ. As a part of the family of God, we ought to welcome those of the Body of Christ into our homes.

At one time I challenged the members of the church, as their pastor, to open up their homes by inviting in, as least once a month, another member of the church that had never been in their home. What a wonderful way it would be to get to better know the members of the church we attend.

Romans 12:9-13 says, "Let love be without hypocrisy. Abhor what is evil; cling to what is good. Be devoted to one another in brotherly love; give preference to one another in honor; not lagging behind in diligence, fervent in spirit, serving the Lord; rejoicing in hope, persevering in tribulation, devoted to prayer, contributing to the needs of the saints, practicing hospitality."

In this passage, practicing hospitality means to entertain strangers. It means to invite people into your home that have not been there before. I know how we are. We get into our little groups, and there is nothing wrong with that for we are drawn to people who have common interests. Some are golfers; some ride motorcycles, some fish, some do whatever it is they do. We gather together with those who like doing the things we do. There is nothing wrong with spending time with those who have common interests. But we need to resist that which becomes a mold out of which we cannot break. We need to be stretched and pulled out of our comfort zones, for we are called to open up our arms and our homes to strangers as well as those we already know.

Of the members of the early church, Acts 2:46 says, "Day by day continuing with one mind in the temple, and breaking bread from house to house, they were taking their meals together with gladness and sincerity of heart..."

One of the chief witnesses of the early church was hospitality. It literally oozed out of them. They spent time with one another, not just on the Sabbath. They went from house to house, breaking bread with one another and got to know one another. We know of no better way to get to know someone than sitting around a meal shared in love.

Have you ever invited someone for dinner and the conversation around the kitchen table bubbles so sweet that you never made it to the living room or the family room for the entire evening? This happens often at our house.

Recently, my wife and I we were invited to a home for dinner and arrived at 6:00 p.m. Before we knew it, it was 10:00 p.m. and we never left the dining room table. For four hours we shared not only a wonderful meal but also an evening of talking about our wonderful Lord Jesus. What a night!

The Bible encourages us to "practice" hospitality. It does so because if we do not make plans to do it, we won't do it. We have to will to do it then practice again and again.

Let me share with you what John Wesley called his rules for life:

Do all the good you can.

By all the means you can.

In all the ways you can.

In all the places you can.

To all the people you can.

As long as ever you can.[2]

Brothers and sisters, we have been admonished to encourage one another, build up one another, comfort one another, care for one another, serve one another, show hospitality to one another, and can I add, for as long as we can.

Questions to Ponder

Read 1Thessalonians 5:11

Are there areas in your life where you seem to flourish when encouraged by others?

What are some ways that your family and friends would benefit by your words of encouragement?

Read 2 Corinthians 1:3-5 and 1 Corinthians 12:24-26

Describe a personal experience in which you received comfort from God that you were able to pass on to another.

When have you experienced 1 Corinthians 12:26?

Read Galatians 5:13 and I Peter 4:9

If you are a bond-servant of Jesus, what should be the attitude of your heart in regards to serving others?

How can you become more intentionally hospitable in your home?

Personal Application

Pray that God may open your eyes to those around you who need a word of encouragement and that He will also give you the courage to encourage them.

As an individual, are you more apt to encourage and build up members of your family before others or is it the other way around?

Read Matthew 20:25-28, and then pray that God would give you the heart of a servant and show you how and where to exercise that gift.

What stops you from inviting someone into your home that you might share God's gift of hospitality with them?

Chapter 9

CLOTHE YOURSELVES WITH HUMILITY TOWARDS ONE ANOTHER

—ɯ—

Concerning humility, the Apostle Peter wrote, "Therefore, I exhort the elders among you, as your fellow elder and witness of the sufferings of Christ, and a partaker also of the glory that is to be revealed, shepherd the flock of God among you, exercising oversight not under compulsion, but voluntarily, according to the will of God; and not for sordid gain, but with eagerness; nor yet as lording it over those allotted to your charge, but proving to be examples to the flock. And when the Chief Shepherd appears, you will receive the unfading crown of glory. You younger men, likewise, be subject to your elders; and all of you, clothe yourselves with humility toward one another, for God is opposed to the proud, but gives grace to the humble" (I Peter 5:1-5).

Paul also speaks to us about humility. "Therefore I, the prisoner of the Lord, implore you to walk in a manner worthy of the calling with which you have been called, with all humility and gentleness, with patience, showing tolerance for one another in love, being diligent to preserve the unity of the Spirit in the bond of peace" (Ephesians 4:1-3).

To the Church at Philippi Paul wrote, "Therefore if there is any encouragement in Christ, if there is any consolation of love, if there is any fellowship of the Spirit, if any affection and compassion, make my joy complete by being of the same mind, maintaining the same love, united in spirit, intent on one purpose. Do nothing from selfishness or empty conceit, but with humility of mind regard one another as more important than yourselves; do not merely look out for your own personal interests, but also for the interests of others" (Philippians 2:1-4).

Paul exhorted the Colossians to put on various character qualities. "So, as those who have been chosen of God, holy and beloved, put on a heart of compassion, kindness, humility, gentleness and patience; bearing with one another, and forgiving each other, whoever has a complaint against anyone; just as the Lord forgave you, so also should you" (Colossians 3:12-13).

An old hymn of the church says:

Naught have I gotten but I've received,

Grace hath bestowed it since I have believed.

Boasting excluded, my pride I abase,

I'm only a sinner saved by grace.[1]

I want you think about something. What do you have that God, through His mercy and grace, has not given to you? I know we live in a land where everybody thinks they are a self-made man or self-made woman. But I have a surprise for them. James 1:17 says, "Every good thing given and every perfect gift is from above, coming down from the Father of lights..."

From the air we breathe to the talents and the gifts we possess, it has all come from God's loving hand. Fact of the matter is that the gifts God gives to us are not really ours until we give them back and He gives them to us a second time. Then they truly become ours. They all belong to God. Every breath, every material possession, every joy in your life, every good and perfect gift, has come down from Him, the Father of lights. "Not have I've gotten, but what I've received." What do you have that God has not given you?

Humility does not rank high in the world's list of things to strive for. We do not hear much of humility in the media, nor do we see a lot of people striving for humility. I believe one reason that Christians do not strive for humility is that we have a wrong understanding of what humility is. Humility isn't thinking less of oneself, rather humility is just thinking of oneself less. Humility means thinking rightfully and truthfully about oneself. The Bible tells us all we need to know about ourselves, about human nature. We need to believe what God says about us.

The Apostle Paul addressed this issue in his letter to the Christians in Rome. In Romans 12:3, he said, "For through the grace given to me I say to you not to think more highly of himself than he ought to think; but to think so as to have sound judgment, as God has allotted to each a measure of faith."

Do not think more highly of yourself than you ought to think. The Phillips translation says, "Do not cherish exaggerated ideas of yourself or of your importance."[2]

When talking to others as to the importance that we personally hold in God's overall plan, I have given the following illustration. Walk out into the water of a lake or the ocean until the water comes up to your waist. Then walk back to shore, look back towards the water and observe the hole that is left where you were standing. Of course, there is no hole; the water filled in the space you occupied. We could say the same thing as a member of the kingdom of God. The kingdom of God is so all-inclusive that it will open up and make room for us to come in, but if we do not want to play our part, the kingdom of God will not suffer ultimately from our refusal to get into the game. We will not leave a hole in God's plan. We need to be careful that we do not possess exaggerated ideas about our importance, but that we have a sane and biblical estimate of who we are before Christ and before one another.

The man who introduced my wife Sandy and me to Christ was a surgeon of renown in the field of female cancer research. He was also one of the most humble people I have ever met. I remember him saying that he was just a technician who had been trained to cut open a body and remove diseased tissue, approximate that tissue and suture it back together. He was vitally aware that if the God-created processes that help a body to heal did not work, his best work would be for naught. I often heard him say, "I'm just a technician." And yet, here was a man that God set very highly in the field of medicine and cancer research, a man sought out. Yet one day in his humility he dared take a young Navy hospital corpsman and his wife and join them on their knees as he introduced them to the Lord Jesus Christ.

Pride and arrogance filled the heart of the angel Lucifer and got him kicked out of heaven. Of his fall, Isaiah 14:12-14 says, "How you have fallen from heaven, O star of the morning (Lucifer), son of the dawn! You have been cut down to the earth, you have weakened the nations! But you said in your heart, 'I will ascend to heaven; I will raise my throne above the stars of God, and I will sit on the mount of the assembly in the recesses of the north. I will ascend above the heights of the clouds; I will make myself like the Most High."

"I will" was the downfall of Lucifer. Do you see that? Five times in this passage he said, "I will."

Do we ever hear that in our world? Do we hear it in our own minds and coming from our own lips? "I will" and I don't care what you think. "I will" and I don't really care what God thinks. I will, I will, I will.

The famed British minister, F.B. Meyer, said, "I used to think that God's gifts were on shelves, one above the other, and that the taller I grew the easier I could reach them. Now I find that God's gifts are on shelves, but one beneath another, and that the lower I stoop the more I get."[3]

The greatest blessings that God has to offer his children we realize when we humble ourselves before Him and before one another.

Hear what Peter said when he calls us to humble ourselves before one another, "For God is opposed to the proud, but gives grace to the humble" (1 Peter 5:5).

Do you know what that means? God actively resists the proud. Think about it. Would you rather have God actively resisting you and everything you attempt and do, or would you rather have Him pulling for you? God opposes the proud! If we will not humble ourselves God will begin to actively resist our plans. But what does He do to the humble? He pours out his grace. His empowering presence brings to us unmerited favor, his divine blessing and provision.

SUBMIT TO ONE ANOTHER

"Therefore be careful how you walk, not as unwise men but as wise, making the most of your time, because the days are evil. So then do not be foolish, but understand what the will of the Lord is. And do not get drunk with wine, for that is dissipation, but be filled with the Spirit, speaking to one another in psalms and hymns and spiritual songs, singing and making melody with your heart to the Lord; always giving thanks for all things in the name of our Lord Jesus Christ to God, even the Father; and be subject to one another in the fear of Christ" (Ephesians 5:15-21).

The King James version of the Bible says, "...submitting yourselves to one another in the fear of God."

Submit to one another. That's about as hard as humbling ourselves before one another, isn't it? We didn't come wired for this. It takes a supernatural transformation of our hearts and minds. We must be empowered by the Holy Spirit to do these things and to walk in this manner.

The Greek word translated "submit" is the word "*hoopistaso.*" As a military term, it literally means, "To arrange troops in divisions under the command of a leader."

It refers to the ordering of military troops into divisions, battalions and companies. Each one of them has a commander over them, from the division level to the individual squads in each company.

When I joined the United States Navy, I did not get to choose the leaders that they placed over me. When I arrived at Boot Camp I was told that my company commander was Machinist Mate Chief Simpson and that my battalion commander was Lt. J.G. Weigle. I had to memorize these names; I had to know every person in the chain of command from the top admiral on down. These were the ones to whom I was called to submit and I had no choice in the matter.

It's different in Christ's kingdom. As Christians, God calls us to voluntarily submit to one another, to voluntarily subject ourselves to one another.

Each one of us is called to submit to one another. Why does the Lord call us to do this? Because submitting to one another honors the Lord. *The Message* says, "Out of respect for Christ, be courteously reverent to one another."[4] I like that.

"Out of respect for Christ." When I am willing to submit to you and walk in a respectful manner with you, the first thing I'm doing is honoring God. It's an act of worship. A refusal to submit to one another holds Christ in contempt. We don't want to hear that do we?

God didn't call us to see one another in the light of our professions, our social standings, or our gifts, but in the light of Christ. When we see one another in the light of Christ, we will also see the true dignity of every person, all created in the image of God. Every person in the Body of Christ has an inherent dignity and an inherent worth, which has absolutely nothing to do with the color of their skin, their education, the size of their house, what kind of car they drive, their bank account, or anything like that. Rather, it has to do with the fact that we are all children of the same heavenly Father, redeemed by the blood of the Lamb, the Lord Jesus Christ.

We submit to one another in an act of worship unto our Lord and our God, whether we start in the home, within the church, or in the society to orders that God has laid out. The home, the church and the state were all God's ideas, the home being the oldest and most sacred. But within God's chosen order, God calls us to submit at some place to someone at some time.

Some may wonder if everyone takes this posture, where does leadership fit in. The Bible makes it very clear concerning an order of leadership within the church. It speaks of elders, deacons, and teachers being part of God's order and part of God's design. We can't successfully carry on ministries within the church without leadership. When the church gives someone the authority to lead, we need to willingly submit to that leadership, even if we think we have a better idea.

Following my service in the Navy, my wife and I returned to our home town in southern Idaho. In a short time we found a new church which we began to attend on a regular basis. After a period of time the pastor said something that didn't sit right with me. And like many do, we left the church and began to search for another. For about the next two months we bounced from church to church looking for that new place to fit, but nothing fit.

In a time of prayer one day, the Lord revealed to me that we should return to the church we had left because that pastor was a chosen instrument of His and would play a significant part in our lives and future ministry. We returned and began to joyfully submit to God and the pastoral authority that he placed over us in that fellowship.

God honored that act of obedience and submission, for within a year I was asked to join the ministry staff of the church and over the next two years was personally discipled at the feet of this pastor. He became in the truest sense of the word, my "spiritual father" in the faith; much like Paul was to Timothy.

Had I been unwilling to submit to God's plan and also to God's man, my growth and ministry would have been greatly impeded. I have come to believe that without submission we will not find an ongoing revelation of God's unfolding plan in our life as a believer. As we obey God and His Word, He reveals Himself to us.

Even as a pastor, God calls me to submit to the other ministry leaders he has placed in the church that I serve. Quite often, God calls me to listen to and to submit to their new and fresh ideas. I am not the only one in the church with vision. I need to recognize that and then give these leaders the freedom to lead where they are gifted.

One of the greatest examples of servant leadership found in the Bible is when, on the night of the Last Supper, Jesus took a basin of water and a towel and washed the feet of his disciples. When he finished that task he sat once again at the table and told his disciples, "…you also ought to wash one another's feet. For I gave you an example that you also should do as I did to you" (John 13:14-15).

Too often, leadership in the world equates to getting to the top at whoever's expense, and once there, to rule with an iron fist. In contrast, leadership in the church means earning the right to lead by showing your willingness to serve. The right to lead in the church is not about diplomas and ordinations, but about serving. We earn the right to lead by showing the body of Christ that we will lay down our lives for them. When you have leaders willing to do that, it makes it a bit easier for you to voluntarily rank under them as you grow in Christ.

Jesus, our prototype, said that He came not to be served but to serve and to lay down his life. He calls us to take up the basin and towel, serving one another in humility, in mutual respect, and to submit to one another.

STIMULATE ONE ANOTHER TO LOVE AND GOOD DEEDS

From the writer of Hebrews, "Therefore, brethren, since we have confidence to enter the holy place by the blood of Jesus, by a new and living way which he inaugurated for us through the veil, that is, his flesh, and since we have a great priest over the house of God, let us draw near with a sincere heart in full assurance of faith, having our hearts sprinkled clean from an evil conscience and our bodies washed with pure water. Let us hold fast the confession of our hope without wavering, for he who promised is faithful; and let us consider how to stimulate one another to love and good deeds, not forsaking the assembling together, as is the habit of some, but encouraging one another; and all the more as you see the day drawing near" (Hebrews 10:19-25).

"Stimulate one another to love and good deeds."

The Greek word translated "stimulate" in this text literally means to provoke. The truth of the matter here—we do not need lessons on how to provoke another. We know how to push one another's buttons, don't we? We know how to get under another's skin. But here the writer calls us to a higher standard of provoking one another. Here the call means to provoke one another to love and good deeds.

Read the same text from *The Message,* "...let us see how inventive we can be in encouraging love and helping out."[5] I like that. How inventive can we be in seeking fresh ways to stimulate one another in good deeds? Beginning in our homes, and then our church, and then in our communities.

I want to remind you of something. None of us has been called to prove ourselves right. Rather, the Lord has called us to prove ourselves in love. If winning the argument matters to you, or if being right matters to you, you will travel a lonely road. God calls us to prove ourselves in love, to get behind one another and help one another to the front of the line. We are called to discover ways to lift up one another to encourage and strengthen them in their faith. This will happen only when we willingly get on our knees and humble ourselves before one another.

This stimulating one another to love and good deeds ranks as one of the main activities of our coming together as the Body of Christ.

From the Old Testament to the New Testament we see God calling his people to join together in the worship of their God. Corporate worship is God's idea; it is His plan, a plan that is twofold. First, we join together to worship our God. Second, we join together to encourage one another in living out our Christian faith.

We live in a world that has the capacity to speak discouragement into our lives in many ways. But it should be different when we gather together with God's people, our family in Christ. In our corporate gatherings we need to lift up and encourage one another, pray *for* and *with* one another. We all face the same challenge of living for Christ in a fallen world. How wonderful to know that brothers and sisters walk at our side, supporting us along the way, encouraging us to carry on. I love the body of Christ. After Jesus and my family, I love the Body of Christ most of all.

One of the greatest visible witnesses of the early church was the fellowship that the early believers had with one another. The Greek word from which "fellowship" is translated shines as a most beautiful word, *koinonea*. *Koinonea* means to be as committed to one another as we are to Jesus. If we commit ourselves to our Lord Jesus, we are called to be just as committed to his body, the church. When we commit ourselves to one another as we do to the Lord, *koinonea* happens. And where *koinonea* happens, the power of the Holy Spirit fills our lives as individuals as well as our corporate gatherings.

Questions to Ponder

Read Luke 14:11, 18:14 and Matthew 18:1-4

Humility is a person's proper estimate of himself in relation to God and others.

How does the world, covertly or overtly, promote pride?

According to Luke, what will Jesus do with the proud? What will he do with the humble?

How does one humble themselves before God so that God does not have to humble them?

Why did Jesus use a child as an example of humility?

How have you personally experienced being humbled?

Read Ephesians 5:21

Submit to one another means to voluntarily rank under another.

Has the world's view of submission tainted your point of view?

How, in practical ways, are we to rank under those given authority in the Body of Christ?

Does submission to church authority mean that we are not free to voice our concerns?

Can you describe a time when you chose, by faith, to live out God's call to submit to another? What were the results?

Read Hebrews 10:23-25

Provoke one another to love and good deeds.

Why are believers exhorted to assemble together?

What will be lost if a believer chooses not to fellowship with other believers on a regular basis?

Personal Questions

Do you know a Christian that you might encourage to be in regular fellowship with the Body of Christ?

What might stop you from regularly fellowshipping with the body?

Do you need to submit to someone but refuse to do so?

Chapter 10

LIVING FREE

In Galatians, Paul contrasts the Law and Works with the true Gospel. "For you were called to freedom, brethren; only do not turn your freedom into an opportunity for the flesh, but through love, serve one another. For the whole Law is fulfilled in one word, in one statement, 'You shall love your neighbor as yourself.' But if you bite and devour one another, take care that you are not consumed by one another. But I say, walk by the Spirit, and you will not carry out the desire of the flesh. For the flesh sets its desire against the Spirit, and the Spirit against the flesh; for these are in opposition to one another, so that you may not do the things that you please. But if you are led by the Spirit, you are not under the Law. Now the deeds of the flesh are evident, which are: immorality, impurity, sensuality, idolatry, sorcery, enmities, strife, jealousy, outbursts of anger, disputes, dissensions, factions, envying, drunkenness, carousing, and things like these, of which I forewarn you, just as I have forewarned you, that those who practice such things will not inherit the kingdom of God. But the fruit of the Spirit is love, joy, peace, patience, kindness, goodness, faithfulness, gentleness, self-control; against such things there is no law. Now those who belong to Christ Jesus have crucified the flesh with its passions and desires. If we live by the Spirit, let us also walk in the Spirit. Let us not become boastful, challenging one another, envying one another" (Galatians 5:13-26).

This passage of scripture sets before us the contrast of a life lived in the flesh and life lived in the power of the Spirit of God. Paul presents to us two lists of character qualities. The first list identifies the deeds of the flesh, those things the unredeemed human nature tends to do without effort or lessons. The second list, called the Fruit of the Spirit, is the very character qualities of Christ manifested in the life of the believer through the indwelling power of the Holy Spirit.

When one is born anew of the Spirit, they become instantly aware of a dynamic tension in their lives. Something has changed! They now become aware of internal wrestlings as the desires of the flesh and the desires of the Spirit fight face-to-face.

The British poet, Studdert Kennedy wrote, "I am a man, and a man's a mixture, right down from his very birth; for part of him comes from heaven and part of him comes from earth."[1]

Nowhere is this confession truer than in the life of one who has been born again. The desires of the Spirit that now grow in them run contrary to the desires of their flesh. Verse 17 says, "For the flesh sets its desire against the Spirit, and the Spirit against the flesh; for these are in opposition to one another, so that you may not do the things that you please."

Before I surrendered my life to Christ, I did my own thing. The desires of the world, the flesh and the devil ruled my life. I was not aware of any struggles with temptation; I fulfilled the lusts by living out the deeds of the flesh. Eat, drink, and be merry was the motto I lived by. During that time the Schlitz Brewing Company had a commercial that said, "You're only going around once so grab for all the gusto you can." "Gusto Grab-bing" was my chief pursuit of life.

Then one January night in 1972, I surrendered my life to the Lord Jesus Christ, and everything changed. Immediately, I began to experience what verse 17 was all about. The desires of my flesh worked in opposition to the desires of the Holy Spirit who had now come into my life.

The apostle Paul in verse 13 says we have been called to freedom, and for Paul, Christian freedom did not mean freedom to indulge the lower side of our nature, but freedom to walk in the power of the Spirit.

The call to freedom leads us to the freedom to walk in the power of the life of the Spirit of God. Our lives are no longer constrained by the rules of the law chiseled in stone, but by the love of Christ who now writes his law on our hearts. We begin to desire the things that He desires and to love the things that He loves. We become new creatures feasting on the good things of God. And when we feast on the good things of God the Fruit of the Spirit begins to emanate from our lives. The Fruit of the Spirit increases and the deeds of the flesh begin to diminish.

When we walk in the Spirit and cooperate with the Spirit, the very character qualities of the Lord Jesus Christ will be reproduced in our lives by the Spirit of God that now lives within us.

If it were possible for you to physically hang out with Jesus for the next few days, you would sense emanating from His being, love, joy, peace, patience, kindness, goodness, faithfulness, gentleness and self-control.

The truth of the matter, you do have the opportunity to hang out with Jesus. You hang out with Him when you study His Word, when you pray, and when you fellowship with other believers.

The Fruit of the Spirit is not produced in the life of the believer through self effort but rather by surrendering one's life to Christ and then abiding in him. Jesus told us how in John 15.

"I am the true vine, and My Father is the vinedresser. Every branch in Me that does not bear fruit, He takes away; and every branch that bears fruit, He prunes it so that it may bear more fruit. You are already clean because of the word which I have spoken to you. Abide in Me, and I in you. As the branch cannot bear fruit of itself unless it abides in the vine, so neither can you unless you abide in Me. I am the vine, you are the branches; he who abides in Me and I in him, he bears much fruit, for apart from Me you can do nothing. If anyone does not abide in Me, he is thrown away as a branch and dries up; and they gather them, and cast them into the fire and they are burned. If you abide in Me, and My words abide in you, ask whatever you wish, and it will be done for you. My Father is glorified by this, that you bear much fruit, and so prove to be My disciples. Just as the Father has loved Me, I have also loved you; abide in My love. If you keep My commandments, you will abide in My love; just as I have kept My Father's commandments and abide in His love. These things I have spoken to you so that My joy may be in you, and that your joy may be made full" (John 15:1-11).

In his first epistle, the Apostle John tells us that we can experience no life in the Spirit unless we abide in Christ. This abiding life is the fruitful life, the joy filled life and the powerful life. We need to understand what abiding means.

To abide means to dwell with or to be continually present. It means coming into another's house, unpacking your suitcase and staying awhile. Christ asks the believer to abide in Him, to enter into His family, to enter into His household and stay.

As branches of a tree can bear fruit only if they stay attached to the tree, a believer can bear fruit only by staying attached to Jesus. He said that if we will abide in Him we will not only be fruitful but we will produce fruit that will remain, not just for the moment but even into eternity.

The branches of a fruit tree do not produce fruit through self effort, but simply abide and feed off the life-giving sap of the tree. Branches simply absorb the life-giving sap that comes up from the roots, flows through the vine and makes the branches bear fruit. Christ alone is our root; He is the vine to which we are attached. In that relationship, the life-giving essence, the Spirit of God who dwells in Christ, now dwells in the believer, making them fruitful with the fruit that filled the life of Christ Himself.

If you and I will abide in Christ and make room for Him by spending time with Him alone, spending time with others who love and serve Him, we will begin to produce fruit as well, and it will not be fruit that is born through sweat and effort, but will be fruit produced because the very sap that flows through the vine, Christ Jesus our Lord, will be the sap that will flow through us, the branches. It is impossible to hang around Jesus and not be changed. The power of the Holy Spirit guarantees that.

What does He ask of us? That we abide in Him, that we would be changed by the life-giving sap of the vine, the Holy Spirit that lives within us. This happens as we pray and study His word and fellowship with His children. In this abiding, the fruit of Christ manifests in our lives.

We have considered 29 admonitions concerning the posture that Christians ought to take before one another—how we ought to rank, speak, to talk about and act toward one another. Let's review this list once again.

Love one another

Forgive one another

Pray for one another

Confess your sins to one another

Bear one another's burdens

Be devoted to one another

Give preferences to one another

Regard one another as more important than yourself

Do not speak against another

Do not complain against another

Do not judge one another

Accept one another

Show tolerance for one another

Bear with one another

Be kind to one another

Be of the same mind to one another

Teach one another

Admonish one another

Speak to one another in psalms, hymns and spiritual songs

Speak truth to one another

Encourage one another

Build up one another

Comfort one another

Care for one another

Serve one another

Be hospitable to one another

Clothe yourselves with humility toward one another

Submit to one another

Stimulate one another to love and good deeds

EPILOGUE

In closing, I want to share with you the reason I believe that we are called to submit our lives to the twenty nine one another admonitions found in the New Testament.

Listen closely to these words from the writer of Hebrews. "Let us hold fast the confession of our hope without wavering, for He who promised if faithful; and let us consider how to stimulate one another to love and good deeds, not forsaking the assembling together, as is the habit of some, but encouraging one another; and all the more as you see the day drawing near" (Hebrews 10:23-25).

Why are we encouraged not to forsake the assembling together of the Body of Christ? It is because our faithful involvement with the Body of Christ is God's chosen strategy to conform us to the image of His Son.

As Christians, we were saved by the sovereign work of the Lord Jesus Christ. Concerning our salvation we have nothing of which we can boast (Ephesians 2:8-9).

After being saved God placed each of us within a new family called the Body of Christ, His Church. There, along with other fellow believers, we begin to grow in Christ. Much to our surprise not everyone in the church is perfectly loving and kind and generous and gracious. In fact, the truth be told, we all at one time or another have been rubbed the wrong way or deeply offended by a brother or sister in Christ. We find that there are rough edges in the body, edges that irritate and bruise. At times, the temptation to forsake the assembling of the saints is great. Yet it is these very saints, the loving ones and the not so loving ones that God uses to shape us and mold us to be like Jesus. "How so?" you might ask.

When I was growing up in rural Southern Idaho, there were many "Rock Hounds" in the area. These individuals spent hours on end combing the countryside for various kinds of rocks. After a day of collecting they would take their new assortment of rocks home and place them in a rock tumbler.

The rock tumbler was not only filled with other rocks but also an abrasive grit. When the machine was turned on the rocks and the grit tumbled together, often for days at a time. The finished product that came out of that tumbler in no way resembled the rocks that went in. The dull and rough exteriors of the untumbled rocks had been transformed to smooth and shiny surfaces that allowed the inner beauty of the rocks to come forth. Upon handling and looking at the finished rocks one would have never guessed that such beauty lay below the surface of the rocks that went into the tumbler. The Body of Christ is like that rock tumbler.

In chapter one I quoted Oswald Chambers who said, "God does not make us holy in the sense of character; He makes us holy in the sense of innocence; and we have to turn that innocence into holy character by a series of moral choices" (*My Utmost for His Highest, September 8*).

Though washed in the Blood of the Lamb and made new at our new birth in Christ, there is yet a maturation process ahead of us by which God shapes and molds our character. The Body of Christ is the arena of that shaping. It is through the Spirit empowered applications of the one another admonitions that we learn to love as Christ loved, forgive as Christ forgave, and lay down our lives for one another as He laid down His life for us. Though everything in us at times wants to run from and avoid those who rub us the wrong way, it is as we stay engaged with one another that we are shaped and molded and changed from glory to glory into the image of Christ (II Corinthians 3:18).

When a preacher proclaims, "...do not forsake the assembling together as is the habit of some," it is not a ploy to fill the seats of the sanctuary from Sunday to Sunday; it is a call to submit God's great shaping tool so that from you will emanate the very beauty of Christ.

The writer of Hebrews also told us that though Christ was a Son, He learned obedience through the things that He suffered (Hebrews 5:8). Like Christ, His bride will not be perfected by lying on a bed of ease or having everything her way. She too will be tested and tried like the rock in the tumbler. If she is faithful she will come out as pure gold.

My dear brothers and sisters in Christ, may God open your eyes so that you may see just how much you need your brothers and sisters in Christ. They are, every one of them, a vital part of God's strategy to conform you to the image of His Son. Ask the Holy Spirit to make this reality real to your heart.

"For just as we have many members in one body and all the members do not have the same function, so we, who are many, are one body in Christ, and individually members of one another" (Romans 12:4-5).

Endnotes

Introduction

1. Me and Jesus by Tom T. Hall, 1971
2. Oswald Chambers, My Utmost for His Highest, October 10 (Discovery House Publishers, Grand Rapids, MI, 1992)

Chapter One

1. Oswald Chambers, My Utmost for His Highest, September 8

(Discovery House Publishers, Grand Rapids, MI, 1992)

1. C.S. Lewis, Mere Christianity, Pg 86 (Macmillan Publishing Company, New York, N.Y. 1977)

Chapter Two

1. Oswald Chambers, My Utmost for His Highest, September 8 (Discovery House Publishers, Grand Rapids, MI)

2. Paul Lee Tan, The Encyclopedia of Illustrations, p. 459 (Assurance Publishers, Rockville, MD)

3. Charles Colson *Who Speaks for God?* Pg. 121 (Crossway Books, Winchester, IL 1985)

4. *To End All Wars*, Ernest Gordon (Harper Collins Publishers, New York, NY 2002).

5. Paul Lee Tan, The Encyclopedia of Illustrations, p. 459 (Assurance Publishers, Rockville, MD)

Chapter Three

1. *1. The Message*, translated by Eugene Peterson (NavPress Publishing Group, Colorado Springs, Co 1994)

2. *2.* Franklin Graham & Jeanette Lockerbie, Bob Pierce...This One Thing I Do, Pg 77 (Word Books, Waco, Texas 1983)

Chapter Six

1. Matthew Henry, The Bethany Parallel Commentary on the New Testament, Pg. 1144 (Bethany House Publishers, Minneapolis, MN 1983)

Chapter Eight

1. Life's Scars by Ella Wheeler Wilcox, The Best Loved Poems of the American People by Hazel Felleman, p. 645 (Doubleday, New York, 1936)

2. John Wesley: Leader of the Methodists Movement, Christian History & Biography, Issue 2, 1983 (Christianity Today, Carol Stream, IL)

Chapter Nine

1. *1.* Only a Sinner by James M. Gray, 1851-1935
2. *2.* J.B. Phillips Translation
3. F.B. Meyer, Topical Encyclopedia of Living Quotations, Pg. 102 (Bethany House Publishers, Minneapolis, MN 1982)
4. The Message, translated by Eugene Peterson (NavPress Publishing Group, Colorado Springs, CO 1994)
5. Ibid.

Chapter Ten

1. Studdert Kennedy, From a Woodbine Willey Poem, William Barclay, The Letters to the Galatians and Ephesians, Pg. 46, (The Westminster Press, Philadelphia, PA 1976)

CPSIA information can be obtained at www.ICGtesting.com
Printed in the USA
BVOW04s0909031114

373282BV00001B/1/P

9 781619 964921